Scholasticism

Scholasticism

Personalities and Problems of Medieval Philosophy

Josef Pieper

Translated by Richard and Clara Winston

ST. AUGUSTINE'S PRESS
South Bend, Indiana

3 4 5 6   18 17 16 15 14 13 12 11

Library of Congress Cataloging in Publication Data
Pieper, Josef, 1904–
[Scholastik. English]
Scholasticism: personalities and problems of medieval
philosophy / by Josef Pieper
[translated by Richard and Clara Winston]
p. cm.
Originally published: New York: Pantheon Press, c1960
Includes bibliographical references (p.) and index
ISBN 1-58731-750-8 (alk. paper)
1. Scholasticism. I. Title
B734.P513 2001
189'.4 – dc21   2001019389

ST. AUGUSTINE'S PRESS
www.staugustine.net

CUIUS IN HORTULO

HUNC CONSCRIPSI LIBELLUM

FAUSTA PER QUINQUE LUSTRA CONIUNCTAE

CONIUGI DULCI

CONTENTS

PREFACE

While it is true that the title of this book does not proclaim it a comprehensive treatise on the personalities and problems of medieval philosophy, it may be well to state this more directly. We have not tried for historical completeness. Had this been our aim, it might justly be objected that a number of personalities of real importance (for example, Roger Bacon, Bonaventura, Raimundus Lullus) have been passed over, or at least scanted.

Nevertheless the book deals with a clearly defined, unitary, and "rounded" subject. This subject is the enduring problem which through all eras has lain hidden behind that technical term so weighed down by a variety of misinterpretations: scholasticism. *And our thesis is that this problem was attacked in a paradigmatic fashion by medieval philosophy, that is to say, in a manner which in no single case can be repeated or imitated, but that nonetheless directly concerns the philosophical-minded Christian of today—and not only him. We want, of course, also to give some picture of the lively intellectual life of the centuries between Boethius and William of Ockham. But our description of the past fundamentally aims at bringing out the inexhaustible contemporaneity of the Middle Ages in regard to this question.*

It may seem surprising that none of the following chapters deals specifically with Thomas Aquinas, although he is constantly mentioned. There are two reasons for this. On the one hand, we attempt to show how the varieties of intellectual materia, *streaming toward a central point from many different sources before Thomas Aquinas, and very soon after his time scattering again in many directions, were for a brief, scarcely measurable moment of history organized in a single recognizable framework by the "universal teacher's" astonishing capacity for order. On the other hand, the resultant gap in the center of the book has been deliberately left, like a planned hollow space; this "vacuum" has already been filled by the account of St. Thomas' personality and thought in another book.[1]*

The present work aspires to be no more than an introduction which assumes and gratefully builds upon the results of scholarly research into the history of scholasticism.

J. P.

. . . the Gospel, that imperishable guide of true wisdom. When reason completes her speculations, she finds that her conclusions coincide with this guide. When, moreover, reason has covered her entire course, much that she sought still remains in darkness; she needs new light and fresh instruction, and draws both from the Gospel.

—Immanuel Kant

I

When we nowadays use the term "Middle Ages," we are not particularly conscious that this name was originally a term of opprobrium. Similarly, we no longer find anything objectionable in calling the cathedrals of Paris and Cologne "Gothic," although that word was originally equivalent to "barbarian." *Media aetas, medium aevum*[1] —four centuries ago these phrases were intended to express contempt. They signified the "middle period," a time of waiting in which nothing of importance happened, an era without qualities of its own, an intermezzo, as opposed to two ages which did have intrinsic qualities: Greco-Roman antiquity and "Modern Times." Such language expressed an epoch's opinion of itself; it was generally meant to imply that really nothing at all had happened in between antiquity and the revival, the "Renaissance" of antiquity. Thus the inscription on Descartes's grave at Saint-Germain-des-Prés in Paris boasts that he was the "refounder of science" (*reconditor doctrinae*) and the first man to defend the rights of human reason. Not the first man in all history, of course, but the first since the downfall of the ancient world.

This judgment of the Middle Ages, above all of its philosophy and science, persisted for a long time. As late as the nineteenth century we find Hegel in his *Lectures on the History of Philosophy* declaring that in order to "move on" quickly he will skip over the thousand years between the sixth and the seventeenth century, will "put on seven-league boots."[2] And when he has at last sped successfully on to Descartes, he declares that now he can "cry land like the sailor"[3]; for it would "be asking too much of anyone" to study the philosophy of the Middle

Ages "by autopsy," since "it is as prolix as it is paltry, terribly written and voluminous."[4] However, in those same first decades of the nineteenth century the pendulum forthwith swung sharply to the other side, to indiscriminate overestimation of everything medieval on the part of the Romantics.

Nowadays all this is more or less forgotten—happily. At least we are in the novel position of being able to confront the concept of "the Middle Ages," and especially the personalities and problems of medieval philosophy, without awkwardness or bias, without prejudgments pro or contra. One principal reason for this happy state of ours is the tremendous work of research which has for several decades been devoted to exploration of this era.[5]

All things are given their form by their boundaries. To perceive the form, we must contemplate the boundaries which set them off from the other forms around them. If medieval philosophy possesses a true historical form of distinct character, that form will appear most plainly if we turn our eyes upon the boundaries which mark off the medieval from the nonmedieval, from what came before and what came afterward. In other words, we must ask ourselves where lie the beginning and the end of medieval philosophy, and of the Middle Ages altogether.

It is naturally impossible to set any specific time, to give any particular date, for the *beginning* of the Middle Ages. Nevertheless, a year can be mentioned which possesses a special symbolic significance. It is A.D. 529. Hegel, too, mentions this as the year in which there occurred, as he puts it, "the downfall of the physical establishments of pagan philosophy."[6] In the year 529 a decree of the Christian Emperor Justinian closed the Platonic Academy in Athens, which had functioned there under the same name for nine hundred years. That same year there took place another event which Hegel does not mention: the founding of Monte Cassino by St. Benedict. That is to say, between Rome and Naples, on a mountain perched high above one of the highways of the great migrations, the *Völkerwanderung,* there arose the first Benedictine abbey. Here, then, we find something very much like a visible boundary where a dying and a new-born age touch one another. Indeed, these contrasting events have a variety of meanings which it will prove worth our while to trace, for not all are apparent on the surface.

In speaking of the downfall of *pagan* philosophy, Hegel expressed the decisive factor: that in the Middle Ages Christian philosophy was ranged against pagan. A more radical polarity cannot easily be conceived. This division is incomparably sharper than the caesura separating, say, Ionian natural philosophy from that of Socrates and Plato. The step from Thales to Socrates, or from Plato to the Stoa, cannot be compared with the step from Thales, Socrates, Plato, and the Stoa on one hand, to Origen, Augustine, Anselm, and Thomas on the other hand. For in the latter case a particular event intervened between the two epochs—an event not in the realm of ideas and concepts, but in the historical realm; not in the sphere of definitions of reality, but in the sphere of reality itself.

Of course there were also historical events of revolutionary importance in the period between Plato and the Stoa; and of course the confusions and uncertainties which followed upon the collapse of Alexander's empire exerted tremendous influence upon philosophical thinking about human existence. But the historical event between antiquity and the Middle Ages, the event we mean here, is of such character that in itself it necessarily had to affect and transform all cogitation about reality in general and about the meaning of human life. Which in turn means that it had to shake philosophy to the foundations—so that medieval philosophy cannot be conceived purely as a continuation (paltry or glorious, according to the point of view) of classical philosophy. Nor as a mere "new era" in the history of human thought.

It should be clear by now that I am speaking of the event which in the technical language of theologians is referred to as the "incarnation." It is quite evident that positions of basic principle inevitably come to the fore when this is mentioned. We do not need to discuss these positions here. However, it must be clear that for the understanding of medieval philosophy it is not a matter of indifference whether a person says, "All history goes to Christ and comes from Him" (these are the words in which Karl Jaspers paraphrases Hegel's underlying conception[7])—or whether he holds, as does Jaspers himself, that the "profoundest caesura" and the "axis of world history" lies "in the intellectual process which took place between 800 and 200 B.C.": the almost simultaneous appearance upon the world scene of Lao-tse, Confucius, the Buddha, Zarathustra, Isaiah, Parmenides, Heraclitus, and Plato.[8] We must realize how impossible it is to understand any medieval author if we do not consider one of the fundamentals of his thinking about the universe and man: his utter conviction that the event of the incarnation made accessible a truth which possesses a power to reveal reality transcending any human insight, and which very precisely concerns the subject matter of the philosopher's thinking.

The question might be raised: Ought we, then, not equate the boundary of "medieval" thought with the beginning of the Christian era itself? In point of fact Gilson's *History of Christian Philosophy in the Middle Ages* does begin with a discourse on the doctrines of the New Testament.[9] Nevertheless, I believe that it makes sense to speak of a Christian era within classical antiquity, and to view Augustine, and certainly Justin or Clement of Alexandria, as belonging to antiquity in spite of their Christianity; as being premedieval thinkers.

In mentioning these men we touch upon a second significant element that lies hidden within the events of that boundary year 529, or to be more precise, in the change of scene from the Athens of the Platonic Academy to the Benedictine abbey on the highway of the migrations.

Augustine, his listeners, and his readers were still living completely within the framework of the *Imperium Romanum,* in the sphere of Hellenistic thought which had been shaped by Neo-Platonism, the Stoa, and Epicurus. That was their intellectual home. To Augustine himself and to all with whom he dealt, Rome was nothing less than the symbol of order in the world. Hence the tremendous wave of shock produced by Alaric's conquest of the city of Rome (A.D. 410), and the resultant elaboration of the historico-theological conception of the "City of God." Although the shell protecting the life of Greco-Roman antiquity was already imperilled, to Augustine it still enclosed the entire world with which his mind was concerned. When the Vandals besieged his episcopal seat of Hippo, he was already a dying man.

Barely a hundred years later, the situation was already totally changed. Boethius, for example, likewise lived completely within the political sphere of the Roman Empire and grew up in the intellectual ambience of classical philosophy; but that was not at all true for his listeners and readers. For Boethius was dealing with the Goths of Theodoric's kingdom; *they* were the new *dramatis personae*.

This change of emphasis is reflected, it would seem, in the contemporary observer. When we think of "Augustine dying in the city besieged by the Vandals" we are still involuntarily regarding matters with the eyes of Augustine, with Roman eyes, that is, and not from the point of view of the Germanic conquerors, although in a certain sense "they" are "we ourselves." On the other hand, when we speak of Boethius and his activities in the Gothic realm, our point of view is no longer so clear. Do we feel more closely linked to Boethius or to Theodoric, King of the Goths? Involuntarily, that is, we are beginning to see with the eyes of the new nations which are overrunning the *Imperium Romanum*. When we go further and think of Alcuin or Hrabanus Maurus, there is no longer any question about it: we have completely changed our inner allegiance.

It seems to me that the turning point lies precisely on that boundary line which separates antiquity from the Middle Ages. Medieval *philosophy* in particular was an affair of those peoples who penetrated into the ancient world from the North. And Boethius, who died a few years before 529, was the first to turn expressly toward them.

In matters of the mind, of course, it remains impossible to speak of a clean dividing line. It could be demonstrated, for example, that Augustine in many ways had already formulated the principles of medieval philosophy. Nevertheless, in his historical existence he remained a premedieval man, a thinker who belonged to antiquity.

In terms of place, as well, the center of intellectual life shifted. Again, we see the change taking place in the time of Boethius. Instead of Athens, Alexandria, Antioch, and Carthage we have the court of Theodoric (Ravenna, Verona, Pavia), the court of Charlemagne, the cities of Canterbury, Paris, Oxford, Cologne. Certainly Rome and Italy in general retained their importance; but the Italy was one occupied by Germanic tribal leaders. And although Thomas Aquinas would be a South Italian, he would have a Norman mother and his native town would be part of the Hohenstaufen kingdom of Sicily.

It remains, then, a historical fact that "barbarian" peoples made themselves at home in a house they had not themselves built. And this fact makes more comprehensible an otherwise troublesome discord which from the very beginning—especially at the beginning—characterized medieval philosophy. Hegel, in spite of the summary haste of his survey, made a very penetrating remark concerning this: "The chief element in the Middle Ages is this division, this duality: two nations, two languages. We see peoples who had previously ruled, who had previously rounded off their own world, their own language, their arts and sciences; and we see the new nations settling down upon this alien foundation. Thus these new nations began with a serious cleavage within themselves."[10] Thus Hegel explains the aspect of scholasticism which so alienated him, the "total confusion of dry reason in the gnarledness of the Nordic-Germanic nature."[11] Upon that Germanic nature, he continues, "the infinite truth of the spirit weighed like a ponderous stone whose tremendous pressure it could only feel but not digest" during those centuries.[12] It is false, and demonstrably false, that the "stone" could not be digested. But on the other hand it is true that the incorporation of something not sprung from native soil, the acquisition of both a foreign vocabulary and a different mode of thinking, the assimilation of a tremendous body of existing thought—that all that was in fact *the* problem which confronted medieval philosophy at its beginnings, and which it had to master. In the very act of mastering it, medieval philosophy acquired its own character.

The new element which distinguishes the Middle Ages from classical, premedieval times, then, can be singled out with some precision. And the point in time which marks its beginning emerges fairly clearly. On the other hand it is obviously far more difficult to distinguish the point in time when the medieval period ended, and the next stage began. Can that be because we have not yet reached that point? Because the Middle Ages are not yet ended?

Actually I think the difficulty arises for the following reason: A new segment of man's history began concurrently with the Middle Ages, but has not ended with the end of the medieval era. The Middle Ages constitute an initial and completed period of this new segment of history; but that segment itself has continued into postmedieval times and into the present "postmodern" era, and will doubtless continue on beyond. Hence the difficulty we have in clearly stating wherein lies the distinguishing "medievalism" of the Middle Ages. For as might be expected, while all of antiquity is definitely over and done with, many "typically medieval" phenomena continue to mark the postmedieval centuries. Thus, for example, it would be rather foolish to maintain that the Christian element in medieval philosophy—which indeed distinguishes it from the thinking of antiquity—is something so specifically medieval that it has forfeited its validity, or even merely its practical force, along with the end of the Middle Ages—in the same way that pagan modes of pre-Christian philosophizing vanished beyond recall with the downfall of the ancient world.

Probably the boundary line marking the end of the Middle Ages can be more distinctly discerned if we keep our eyes fixed upon the second factor we have been discussing. I mean the astonishing fact that the young peoples who penetrated into the Roman Empire from the north should have considered it their task to master and assimilate the accumulated body of tradition they found, including the enormous harvest of patristic theology as well as the wisdom of the ancient world. For only in the light of this fact can we understand one decisive trait of medieval thinking: its "scholarly" aspect—to which, after all, the name "scholasticism" refers. Truly to understand scholasticism, we must bear in mind that it was above all an unprecedented process of learning, a scholarly enterprise of enormous proportions that went on for several centuries. If both the pagan and the Christian heritage of the ancient world were to be truly incorporated, ordering of the existing material undoubtedly came first and foremost. Moreover, that material had to be ordered in terms of being made accessible to teaching and learning. Inevitably, then, the wholly prosaic work of organizing, sorting, and classifying acquired a hitherto unknown importance. And quite naturally the writings of medieval scholasticism lacked the magic of personal immediacy. Schoolbooks leave little room for displays of originality on the part of their authors. Yet it would seem that learning cannot proceed except through schoolbooks. The dissolution of antiquity's world order was indeed taking place during those centuries. And if the major historical task was to acquire the riches of tradition, scholasticism could not but smack of the schoolroom. Its "scholarliness" was not only inevitable but also essential. Who can say whether we would be able, today, to have direct intellectual access to Plato, Aristotle, and Augustine had not the scholastics opened the way with patient spadework? Moreover, the harvest of such an immeasurable body of tradition by the learning and teaching scholastics presupposes an altogether uncommon degree of intellectual autonomy and independence. The intellectual powers of genius, of men like Albertus Magnus and Thomas Aquinas, were required for the task.

What—the question may be raised—does this have to do with the *end* of the Middle Ages, which we are supposed to be discussing? Answer: sooner or later that primarily "learning" attitude would cease to be a vital and pressing concern. The moment had to come. As bit by bit the task of acquisition was accomplished, and as new questions demanded consideration and answers that could only emerge from the direct experience of the "new" peoples, mere preoccupation with existing knowledge had to dwindle in importance, had in the end to be seen as wide of the mark. At the same time, by the later Middle Ages the machinery for acquiring knowledge had been largely institutionalized. Procedures were well established. Although they were meant primarily for exploiting existing stocks of knowledge, it was only natural for those with a vested interest in these procedures to seek to retain them, to continue their dominion.

Ultimately that attempt could lead only to total sterility and dissolution. And that is pretty much what happened. There is no dispute among historians on that score. The end did not descend in the form of an external event, like the closing of the Platonic Academy by imperial decree. Medieval philosophy degenerated from within. Grabmann[13] speaks of a decay setting in precipitately. Gilson says that the end of medieval philosophy can only be described as extreme intellectual confusion and disorder.[14] De Wulf's general history concludes[15] with the statement that scholasticism died not for lack of ideas but for lack of minds.

However, we shall reserve discussion of this "last" act for the final sections of this book.

II

The acquisition of the classical heritage by the peoples of the Germanic North cannot be described by the usual terms of "cultural influence." It was far more—for that heritage was thereby saved from complete oblivion. Had it not been for that acquisition, the discoveries and achievements of the ancient world would largely have vanished from the continuous stream of history. But since the learners were also foreigners taking possession of a stock that had not grown on their own soil and that had been given shape in a language not their own mother tongue, the process of taking over was itself subject to novel conditions. Translation, in the most elemental sense of a carrying over into the recipients' ways of speech and thought; simplification; basic spelling out of things which had simply been taken for granted within the closed sphere of antiquity's traditions—all these processes unexpectedly acquired vital importance. Methodology played a part, of course; but an equal or greater part was played by the initial choice of content. The whole tradition in all its ramifications could not be presented at once. Hence the enormous significance of what was selected first for "translation," what was installed into the foundations of the new structure. A crucial question, too, was whether the right man would turn up to undertake this task. The man who did was *Anicius Manlius Boethius.*

Boethius, curiously enough, is connected with the two "symbolic" events of the year 529, although he did not live to experience them. He had been a pupil of the Platonic Academy, and thus in a sense it was his school which was closed by imperial edict. He was also a contemporary of Benedict of Nursia and, it appears, related to him as a member of the ancient Roman clan of Anicians.

Boethius must be located on the narrow strip of no-man's-land that divides epochs; this historical locus determined his personal destiny. He knew that the world in which he had grown to manhood was doomed; and the world coming into being was not his own, although he would turn passionately to it. Thus he was incontrovertibly at home neither in the old world nor in the new. At first glance, to be sure, no one would seem to be so unquestionably rooted in the soil of antiquity as Boethius, a born Roman and son of a senatorial family, one of the last in his class to finish his education in Athens. But the first glance is deceptive. For in the meanwhile that soil had become "occupied territory." And Boethius, it was plain, did not wish to employ the energies of his mind and heart merely to administer what he had received. He dared to become involved with things new and strange whose future forms were still shrouded in darkness— and turned to the victorious invaders who had conquered the old imperial soil of Italy and were now setting about "learning."

Boethius, that is, went to the court of Theodoric the Goth. There, according to his own testimony, as a young man he soon attained dignities and offices rarely possessed by even old and experienced men. By entering the service of Theodoric, Boethius was placed in a position to "save" and transmit in incomparably effective fashion the intellectual heritage of antiquity. But it is also easy to imagine the perils implicit in this role of mediator, a role which he recognized to be his, and accepted to the full. The mediator is always in danger of being suspected and accused by both sides: as a secret emissary of the enemy power, as a "collaborator," as a traitor. For he cannot be said to be clearly and unambiguously at home on either side.

The atmosphere at Theodoric's court was in any case replete with the elements of conflict. The Gothic King represented himself as the emissary of the Eastern Roman Emperor; but in actual fact he held power as an absolute ruler. Theodoric himself had been raised at the Byzantine court, for he had been a hostage; in his private life, he was partial to Roman customs and Roman ways; his daughter spoke Latin and Greek. At the same time he is credited with the remark that a bad Goth wished to be a Roman, and a bad Roman a Goth. As for the latter, we know that one of the official panegyrics customary at the court, and addressed to several of Theodoric's high dignitaries—Romans, be it noted—praised them for their command of the Gothic language and for raising their children in the Gothic manner.[1] In general, however, Theodoric insisted on clear divisions. No Roman was permitted to hold a leading military post, no Goth an office in the government administration.

Such, then, was the tension-laden world to which Boethius adapted himself: Roman in the service of the Germanic sovereign; "Greek" in the sphere of the Christian religion; Catholic among the Arian Goths. Obviously the situation was rich in interest for a man with a taste for mediation. But it was also fraught with perils, perils of the most authentic sort. And it may be validly stated that in the exercise of his office of mediator, Boethius came to his death.

Now we must discuss this mediatory work in more detail. First and foremost, Boethius was one of the great *translators,* upon whose achievements we have been drawing down to the present day. *Translatio* is certainly one of the recurrent, indispensable, and fundamental forms of all mediation in things of the mind. When we say "universal," we use a word coined by Boethius; likewise when we say "subject" or "speculation" or "define" or "principle." All these are words that Boethius co-ordinated with the Greek of Plato and Aristotle. Strictly speaking, that is the proper business of the translator; he does not create new words, but establishes co-ordinates. In Greek, for example, the word *arché* was a key concept in philosophy from Thales to Aristotle. The word combines two elements of meaning: that of "origin" and that of "rule." Now the word *principium* had always existed in Latin. But that this word, with a similar duality of meaning, should have been co-ordinated with *arché* to stand as its permanent representative—for that we must thank the great translator who can accomplish what is virtually impossible: to transmit thought "safe and sound" from one language to another. We can only marvel at the magnificent precision of the translation of *arché* by *principium*.

The greatness of Boethius as a mediator, however, is to be found not only in this linguistic mastery, this gift for carrying the meaning of the fundamental words unharmed, scarcely changed by transportation, across the frontiers of language. No less magnificent is the way in which he determined what material he was going to "rescue." From the very start he expressly aimed at comprehending the stock of tradition in its entirety. This is not to say that he set himself the task of rescuing every item. That would have been impossible. What he sought was at least the outline of universality—for that alone could give his work an indisputable authority, vis-à-vis the claims to exclusive possession of truth put forward by the adherents of this or that school. Perhaps it was the striving for this all-inclusiveness which gave his work that "indecisiveness" for which Boethius has so often been deprecated.[2] But it also shows how well he must have recognized what was in truth necessary in this era when the continuity of thought was in dire peril. He perceived that preserving the specific doctrines of this or that philosophic school was less important than preserving the common foundation which alone makes possible a variety of philosophic viewpoints. His aim was precisely not to set up an either-or. Although he himself was at bottom a Neo-Platonist, he expressly wanted to preserve both

Plato and Aristotle. Boethius stated this very intention in the highly self-confident sentence: *"Ego omne Aristotelis opus, quodcumque in manus venerit . . . omnesque Platonis dialogos . . . in Latinam redigam formam"*—"I shall translate into Latin every book of Aristotle that comes into my hands, and all the dialogues of Plato."[3] This statement is to be found in a commentary on one of Aristotle's writings on logic—a token, moreover, that Boethius did not content himself with mere translation of texts. In his commentaries, as he tells us in the same passage, he hoped to demonstrate how much agreement there was between Plato and Aristotle in basic philosophical convictions.[4] Presumptuous and probably impossible to perform though such a task was, it is at any rate important that as early as the year 500 Boethius should have laid stress upon Aristotle the *Platonist*—an aspect of Aristotle which has been validated in our day by the researches of Werner Jaeger.

It is not surprising that the grandiloquent plan of translating and interpreting the complete works of Plato and Aristotle was not carried out. It scarcely could have been even if, in Boethius' own words, death had not "prematurely penetrated into the sweetness of the years."[5]

But with his own writings also (including elementary textbooks on arithmetic, astronomy, and music,[6] as well as several theological treatises which we shall discuss below) Boethius long and deeply influenced the future. Six hundred years after his death we find his name mentioned on almost every page of Abélard's treatises on logic.[7] His anonymous influence was perhaps even greater, and that not only as a translator. It is the general rule that the more something is assimilated, the more its tokens of origin are lost. This is true for many of Boethius' intellectual legacies. The carefully delineated concepts of person, fate, eternity (the last being not merely the endless succession of temporal units, but simultaneous possession of everything[8]); the philosophic principle that all knowing necessarily proceeds according to the mode of the knower[9]—for these seeming axioms of philosophy we are indebted to Boethius. The signature of their author has been obliterated because they have long since become common property.

The most important of Boethius' books, the one that indubitably belongs to world literature,[10] was one that he never planned to write. This work, the only one which has always been generally mentioned and remembered in connection with the name of its author, is likewise one which is in no way linked with anything in his previous writings. For the book was forced upon Boethius in terrible fashion.

His life had been one of marvellous expansiveness, of thundering success. Wealth, power, and influence had come to him from everything he touched. By the age of thirty he had risen to the rank of a Roman consul. And suddenly a single, totally unexpected blow descended upon him, casting him from the spaciousness of his existence back upon a tiny cell: to an ultimate, stark encounter with primal reality.

The events are quickly told. Boethius was accused of participation in a conspiracy against Theodoric. He was brought to trial, condemned to death, and in Milan in the year 525 cruelly executed. It was as a prisoner awaiting death that he wrote his book, *The Consolation of Philosophy*. This book revealed a wholly new Boethius— so unlike the Boethius of the theological tracts that for a long time men could scarcely believe that these were written by the same Boethius. (We have spoken of the double role which Boethius must have seemed to play in the eyes of his contemporaries. His personality must have seemed an ambiguous one. This fact had strange reverberations: on the one hand it has been asserted down to most recent times that Boethius was not a Christian at all; and on the other hand he has enjoyed the reputation of being a virtual martyr who suffered death for his faith. Both these hypotheses have been proved false; but it seems to me highly significant that they ever could have been reasonably entertained.)

The Consolation of Philosophy can be read in many different ways. The reader can view it in its purely literary aspect, as a latter-day Platonic dialogue, the imitation of an early work of Aristotle. Or else he can "recognize" in it the model of Dante's *Vita Nuova* and see in its content the doctrines of the Neo-Platonists or the intellectual legacy of the Stoa. The historically trained reader is only too prone to this kind of reading, and he is constantly being encouraged from all quarters to practice it. In the case of the *Consolation* such an approach may lead to many a useful observation. The danger is that it will also prevent the reader from hearing the true voice of Boethius himself, the *vox humana* in the book. To reach out to that, one must be left alone with the book, must shut out distractions and turn the soul's sight and hearing directly upon the actual content. Only then will the true and literal impact of the *Consolatio philosophiae* come through: that here we have a man who has had all the richness of his life's possessions knocked from his hand without warning, and is now trying to answer the question of what is left to him. Face to face with death, this man undertakes to secure his last cash in hand. Only natural that he should consider all the information at his disposal—including the Platonic, Neo-Platonic, Aristotelian, and Stoic doctrines. But he is not in the least concerned with learned citation of famous authors; he is in no mood to manufacture literature. He is concerned with the horribly concrete, life-and-death question of whether the world and existence have now become meaningless to him—yes or no? It is an eternal question of humanity which can enter everyone's life any day. And the answers to it given by Plato or the Stoics are not dismissed as something "historical," for all that the Christian may be able to provide a new, superior, or even final answer.

This last, however, calls for some qualification. It is true that a deeper and truer answer has been offered to the Christian; but that does not yet mean that in practice he has made it his own, that he is capable of making it a reality. Here is one problem that complicates interpretation of *The Consolation of Philosophy*. For Boethius is silent about the Christian answer. This very fact has raised doubts as to whether he was a Christian at all. For if he were, how can it be that in drawing up his accounting, this man in such sore need of consolation does not once expressly mention Christ; that he finds no place for a single thought on the mystery of His Passion? Here is a conundrum which we may possibly never be able to answer. But is it not conceivable that this very silence testifies to Boethius' sincerity and to the completely unliterary seriousness of his profession of faith? In the *Consolatio*, whose style is marked by extreme disillusion ("Everyone has within himself something he does not know as long as he has not searched it out; but if he has searched it out—he shudders"[11])—in this book is also

33

to be found the extraordinary epigram: Nothing can be adorned with adventitious ornaments.[12] What Boethius meant is this: Whatever we "have" becomes our own only if we transform it into ourselves in the innermost chambers of our being; in the final reckoning only what a person "is," not what he "has," counts. Not every thought we are able to conceive, and not every concept that is part of our stock of knowledge, really belongs to us as our own property—no matter how strongly it may appeal to reflective reason and no matter how forthrightly we express our formal agreement with it. In this realm there is endless opportunity for sublime self-deceptions; these disintegrate only when some extreme existential challenge really puts them to the test. A man can very well write—as Boethius did—a highly ingenious book on the Trinity, and yet it may come to light, when life or death is the issue, that he is unable to harvest any fruit, unable to derive any consolation, from such "knowledge." No one can anticipate the final testing, and it alone can reveal to us what really belongs to us and what does not. The extreme situation, in which a man is left only with his true possessions, has laws of its own.

Would it not be possible, I ask myself, for this Athens-educated Roman Boethius to have been a sincere Christian at heart and yet, in that extreme situation, to have found himself "shudderingly" cast back upon an interpretation of life in which the profound consolation of the Christian Mystery remained mute? In no epoch, no matter how "Christian" it may have been, have faith and hope been so readily available to man that he has had only to reach out for them. That is an inexorable fact; it may be forgotten, but it cannot be altered, however much we are on a familiar footing with the divine Mystery in our speech and thought.

The dialogue which forms the center of Boethius' last book, then, is anything but a strained allegory. And none of the interlocutors is an invented, unreal figure. The captive Boethius speaks with the Boethius who is not captive; he holds converse with his own *anima*, which is free because it keeps its gaze fixed upon the divine guarantee of all meaning in this world. Here, incidentally, we have stumbled upon almost the very words of the Boethian definition of spiritual freedom[13] and of philosophy.[14] "Lady Philosophy" who enters the prison cell is therefore not a phantom who declaims alien bookish sentiments; she is not alien at all, but the inner counterpart of the prisoner himself. And that is the greatness of the *Consolatio*: that the tension of this monologue is here in all its strength, is here without any false resolution. The brutal reality of grief, of injustice, of deprivation, will not be put to flight by abstract arguments. On the other hand, the reality of an eternal inviolable order is unsparingly held before the eyes. Neither of the two interlocutors spares the other; but neither silences the other. "If God exists, whence comes Evil? If He does not exist, whence comes Good?"[15] Is it true that Evil "in reality" possesses no Being? ("Are you playing with me? No, this is no game."[16]) If divine Providence dominates history, what about human freedom?[17] Such are the subjects of the discussion. And such is the nature of these questions that not even the most patient efforts can lead to a result. And thus the book cannot end with any spelled-out conclusion. Two of its characteristics make that wholly impossible. The first is Boethius' determination to illuminate his subject to the limits of reason; the second is his refusal to purchase any "solution" by concealing a single difficulty.

Nevertheless, in the end real consolation is found. The

man who has been blinded by griefs sees a new dimension of the world opening before his eyes; and he who has been sunk in lamentation over his losses becomes aware of the infinite riches that are his because of his inclusion in that greater and more real reality.

In the light of all this, it is easily understandable that Boethius should be named among the "founders"[18] of the Middle Ages—if not on account of the effect of *The Consolation of Philosophy*, then for his achievement as translator (in the widest sense), mediator, and commentator. It was Boethius, first and foremost, who laid the groundwork for that protracted process of learning which constitutes the most important strand of medieval intellectual history and which, we have said, makes comprehensible the "scholarly" point of view which is one distinguishing feature of scholasticism. Nevertheless, this is not the reason historians of medieval philosophy generally call Boethius the "first scholastic."[19] The epithet refers to quite another side of his work. For Boethius was the author of a number of small tractates on theological subjects known collectively as the *opuscula sacra*. On the basis of these tractates Boethius is called a "forerunner" of Thomas Aquinas[20]; and the works themselves have been dubbed "first-fruits of the scholastic method."[21]

We must therefore ask what is specifically "scholastic" about these treatises—and may well presume that in exploring this question we shall discover a new aspect of that many-layered concept "scholasticism." In what way, therefore, do Boethius' *opuscula sacra* depart from previous writings of a similar type? He himself, we are told, clearly defined it—for example in the introduction to the tractate on the Trinity. As the title (*Quomodo Trinitas unus Deus ac non tres dii?*) precisely states, the subject is the question: In what sense is the Trinity One God and not three gods? Here Boethius announces his intention to explain this difficult doctrine, which has already been examined many times in the past, only as far as reason will go. This obviously means that his intention is to make convincing, or at least make comprehensible to the rational mind, the dogma of the One God's Trinitarian nature. But how, we may ask, can that be regarded as anything new and revolutionary? Had not Augustine written his great book on the Trinity with the same end in view? Moreover, was not the endeavor to achieve a rational understanding of belief at all times taken for granted—and therefore in no way something distinctively scholastic?

These questions aim incontestably in the right direction. We shall return to them later. Nevertheless it becomes patent that Boethius was undertaking something really new, something that distinguished him from everything which came before. The newness lay in the explicitness of his program; that procedure hitherto practiced *de facto* was consciously presented as a principle. This was done with unequivocal clarity in another of Boethius' tractates—a tractate which is actually no more than a two- or three-page letter dealing with the Trinity (*Utrum Pater et Filius et Spiritus Sanctus de Trinitate substantialiter praedicentur*). The last sentence of this letter addressed to the later Pope John I reads: "As far as you are able, join faith to reason"—*fidem, si poteris, rationemque conjunge.*

New and extraordinary, moreover, was the way in which Boethius carried out this principle of rational examination of dogma. He was wholly consistent; not a single

Bible quotation is to be found in these tractates, even though they deal with virtually exclusively theological subjects. Logic and analysis is all. This was in fact an amazingly new element—which was to be imitated and continued in medieval scholasticism. It is for this that Boethius is called "one of the founders of scholasticism."[22]

We have here, therefore, a comment on the nature of scholasticism. Not that the rationalistic, "non-Biblical" approach is an earmark of scholasticism—although this, too, has often been said,[23] and with some justification. But rather that the conjunction of faith with knowledge, expressly proclaimed by Boethius for the first time, does constitute an earmark of scholasticism. Therefore its specific character is determined (or at least partly determined) by the weight that is ascribed to reason in proportion to faith. We can see, incidentally, that this aspect of scholasticism is much akin to the one already mentioned: "schooling" fits in very well with rationality.

The extent to which rationality did indeed characterize the whole of scholasticism is plain to see throughout. What defined the great age of scholasticism? The fact that its leading minds, Thomas and Bonaventura, say, carried out that co-ordination between believing acceptance of revealed and traditional truth on the one hand and rational argumentation on the other hand with unfailing resoluteness—although they also knew just where to draw the line between the claims of reason and the claims of faith. Bonaventura, too, though by nature more inclined toward the affective and symbolic thinking of mysticism, speaks with great matter-of-factness (likewise in a tractate on the Mystery of the Trinity[24]) of the necessity to grasp by reason, *per rationem*, what has been believed on authority, in so far as that is possible.

It is perfectly evident that such a task is one of extraordinary difficulty, which from the start offers little hope of a permanent solution. Thomas and Bonaventura succeeded in containing the dangerous explosiveness of that conjunction of faith and reason in a contrapuntally structured unity. The very balance of tensions within that unity made for the "rich harvest" of that brief season which we call "high scholasticism." But we may say that the task put a tremendous strain upon the intellects of even such great men as these. They could scarcely have sustained the effort of achieving such a fortunate concord had they not been specially favored by historical circumstances. A new reality, the influx of new experiences, soon dissolved this concord again. Certainly the "synthesis" developed according to the principle set forth by Boethius was not abandoned flightily; it broke down under the impact of these experiences. (And, for good reasons, it has not been possible to reconstruct it down to the present day.) It is, moreover, understandable that for a moment the validity of the principle itself was thrown into question—and this doubt marked the end of the scholastic era and of the Middle Ages altogether. The reversal began when the premise that the "first scholastic" had set up for his program was challenged—both for purposes of argument and out of resignation. The man who might be called the "last scholastic" were he not rather to be counted as one of the first men of the coming era—William of Ockham—was destined to propose a different hypothesis: that belief is one thing and knowledge an altogether different matter; and that a marriage of the two is neither meaningfully possible nor even desirable.

There must be teachers who can gain a hearing for themselves, and pupils who have the capacity and the vital desire to learn. But that is not enough. More is needed if the stock of tradition is to be handed down from generation to generation—and unless this handing down takes place there can be no preservation, let alone enrichment, of the tradition. Also essential is a *school*— the word being understood in the special, original meaning of *scholé*, which means approximately a place for leisure. That is to say, a certain space must be left within human society in which the demands of necessity and livelihood can be ignored; an area which is sheltered from the utilities and bondages of practical life. Within such an enclosure teaching and learning, in general the concern for "nothing but the truth," can exist unmolested.

Diverse societies provide for such "immunity" in diverse ways. In the case of Plato's Academy it was the wealth of a leisure class, the upper crust of a society based on slavery, which guaranteed a free area for philosophizing. The court of Theodoric was also such an enclosure. From the start, however, it carried no promise of being long-lasting. Despite all outward glitter, this court remained fundamentally a kind of armed camp which offered protection and breathing space against the tempests of a politically unsettled world only for a time. Only a decade after the death of Boethius there began a twenty years' war of annihilation, which devastated the country, against the kingdom Theodoric had erected. When the war was over, there were "no longer any Goths in Italy."[25] And another dozen years later the Lombard storm descended upon the victors, again converting the shattered soil of one-time Imperial Rome into a battleground for two or three generations.

When Boethius died, he might still have been confident that Theodoric's new realm had inherited the firmness of Old Rome. His younger fellow official, *Cassiodorus*

—who was to survive Boethius by half a century—could no longer hold to this illusion. And it was Cassiodorus who was to find a new shelter for the work that both men had begun together. For almost a thousand years to come Boethius remained the last "layman" in the history of European philosophy. At the age of fifty, at the peak of his career, Cassiodorus was to leave the world and continue his work henceforth in the isolation of a monastery. That monastery, Vivarium in southern Italy, was founded by Cassiodorus himself.

Like Boethius, Cassiodorus was a Roman by birth, although his family was of Syrian origin. He too went to the court of Theodoric, and rose to a position of high influence there as *magister officiorum*. In the conflict centering around Boethius, Cassiodorus, a clever courtier, seems to have avoided taking any clear position. There are a good many indications that the condemned man felt abandoned by his friend, who had probably also been his pupil. In any case, we know that Cassiodorus later delivered an official panegyric on the accuser of Boethius. But be this as it may, it is no doubt of greater importance that Cassiodorus remained faithful to the task which he and Boethius had begun together. In so doing he too became one of the patriarchs of the dawning era—in the capacity of preserver and transmitter. His real achievement lay not so much in direct instruction as in the realm of administration. Cassiodorus functioned as a kind of minister of education. He conceived the plan, in collaboration with Pope Agapetus, of founding in Rome a university modelled upon those of Alexandria and Nisibis in Syria. This would have been the first university in the Latin West—should the enterprise have succeeded. Its failure, however, was no accident; the prerequisite of political stability was lacking. This very failure was one of the experiences which must finally have decided Cassiodorus to quit his political office. To the diagnostic eye of this statesman and historian[26] it must have become obvious that the public authority was no longer capable of protecting the intellectual heritage; that for the latter's preservation and administration an altogether different type of sheltered enclosure must be found. In those times there simply was no place in which the intellectual life could flourish except the recently founded monastic orders, resting upon the organized humility of a religiously shaped community.[27] "We could not deny it if we would," writes Johann Adam Möhler[28]; "in those days no plant would thrive except one that germinated and grew in the cloister." Not without a note of deprecation has it been said that Cassiodorus' step transferred antiquity's culture from the broad forum of the world into the narrow cell of the Middle Ages. But indeed his move to the isolation of Vivarium represented an act of salvation and of beginning anew. For Cassiodorus brought with him into the monastery his enormous library, which seems to have included the whole literature of Greco-Roman letters, philosophy, and history. And it was he who founded the monastic custom of translating and copying classical texts —with the result that almost the entire stock of classical literature we know today, including the distinctly profane comedies of Plautus and Terence, was preserved and handed down through the work of the monastic scriptoria in the early Middle Ages.

Cassiodorus also undertook writings of his own, again with the aim of rescuing what he could of the intellectual heritage of his time from oblivion. His two-part work, which is usually cited by the abbreviated title of *Institutiones,* sets down the elements of both the theological disciplines and the seven liberal arts. To tell the truth, scarcely a trace of original thinking may be found in the *Institutiones.* The book seems to be simply a collection of the tables of contents of other books, a mere cataloguing of chapter headings, definitions, and subdivisions. And this is not a false impression, not at all; this is what it verily is. For odd as it strikes us, it was precisely this which was necessary at the time. It is as if a man who is planning or sees the inevitability of a headlong flight from his home were to make notes, with telegraphic brevity, as an aid to memory for later on. Taken in themselves, such notes seem neither eloquent nor interesting. Their value can be judged only by one who is capable of seeing them in relation to the former state of affairs, of which they are reminders and notations, and in relation to the future in which they will be used and will bear fruit. Perhaps it is not so irrelevant for us today to consider the form in which the heritage was once saved—and possibly may again have to be saved in the future. Evidently at times the only recourse is to preserve the treasures that have been entrusted to us and to pass them on in the form of uninspiring, apparently withered seed-corn which looks like a handful of dust. But what it looks like is not important. The real question is whether it is seed capable of germination, which someday, under new and more favorable conditions, will be able to shoot forth green sprouts and come to fruition again.

Such was very much the case with Cassiodorus' *Institutiones.* True, he was not much more than a mere compiler and collector; but as a collector he had an eye for value. Thus his *Institutiones* became a source book and mine of information for the following centuries. Without this stock of viable seed, there could scarcely have been the great schoolmasters Alcuin and Hrabanus Maurus, for example. The same is true of a number of the classical concepts of philosophy, which after all were never intended as mere abstract designations, but in every age were destined to keep alive the range of human perception. That philosophy is cognition of divine and human things, in so far as our minds can grasp them; that it is the science of sciences; that it is contemplation of death and learning how to die; that it is attainment of the greatest possible similarity to God—such definitions as these are to be found preserved in the *Institutiones* in the form of concise cue phrases.[29] And if in this way meditations on the nature of the philosophical act by Pythagoras, Plato, Aristotle, the Stoa, Cicero, Seneca, the Neo-Platonists, Augustine, and the School of Alexandria were saved from oblivion, that again we owe to none other than that faithful husbander on the threshold of the Middle Ages: Cassiodorus.

III

From the beginning medieval scholasticism was threatened by an internal peril, one arising from the very nature of its tenets. The peril can be summed up in a single word: rationalism. It was necessary to keep this in bounds. This, then, was done from the beginning, by strange and somewhat daring devices. The conjunction of reason and faith which Boethius had proclaimed, the argument that believers must attain to a rational understanding of the revealed word of God—this principle obviously is based upon a profound explicit confidence in man's natural intellectual powers. Of course this confidence can mean many things, and indeed a great many different things have always been meant by "rational understanding" of the content of faith. It is clear that without a degree of understanding, faith itself, as an act of the human being, could not be held. No one can give credence to an absolutely incomprehensible message; and one who had not grasped what was being talked about would be unable to receive and believe the direct word of God Himself. "Rational understanding" of the substance of belief is indispensable to the extent that the believer must "know" what the divine speech is all about.

It is something else again to demand that divine revelation be made so wholly accessible by rational investigation that its character as mystery is simply abolished. For then both revelation and faith become superfluous. This is what I term "rationalism"; within it lies the assertion that there cannot be anything which exceeds the power of human reason to comprehend.

The great thinkers of medieval philosophy emphatically affirm the principle of the conjunction of faith and reason, and embody it in their writings. But their special quality lies precisely in their rejecting any such "rationalistic" claim.[1] (It must be added immediately, however, that their writings contain extremely deceptive formulations which are apt to mislead the unprepared contemporary reader. Thomas Aquinas, for example, often speaks of "proof" [*demonstratio*] where in reality he is trying to develop only a "reason of convenience," an entirely different affair from proof in the modern sense of the word. To develop a "reason of convenience" means nothing more than to show how the truth of faith "accords" and "suits" what we know from our own experience or rational argument.) Nevertheless it must be granted that scholasticism on the whole, by virtue of its basic approach, contained within itself the danger of an over-estimation of rationality, that is, of thinking by way of arguments and conclsuions. This danger plainly emerges from the speculations on the Trinity by Boethius, the "first scholastic." And when we come to the "necessary reasons" from which Anselm of Canterbury derived the history of Salvation[2] the danger has become almost the outstanding factor. If nevertheless the great masters con-trived, as we have said, to conquer and banish it, the reason lies in that corrective which from the beginning was present as a kind of warning. We must now speak of this in greater detail.

We are dealing here with one of the weirdest events in the history of culture. The true name of the protagonist is unknown to this day, although many researchers have labored to discover it. For over a thousand years men were hoodwinked—we may almost say that they wanted to be hoodwinked. The pseudonym behind which this mysterious figure so successfully hid is *Dionysius Areop-agita*. As everyone knows, the name comes from the New Testament; when Paul delivered his sermon on the "unknown God" on the Areopagus in Athens, some Athenians became his followers and converts. Among them was a member of the Areopagus by the name of Dionysius (Acts 17, 34).

Under this name, then, a number of writings have come down to us, several letters and above all books written in Greek: *On the Divine Names, On the Celestial*

Hierarchy, On the Ecclesiastical Hierarchy, On Mystic Theology. The author who calls himself Dionysius purports to be a disciple of Paul the Apostle—which cannot possibly be true. Almost all historians agree that this "Pseudo-Dionysius"[3] was probably a Syrian contemporary of Boethius whose writings must be dated around the year 500. It will probably remain forever an enigma why the author concealed his name and employed obvious fictions by way of making the pseudonym credible (for example, that he witnessed the death of the Virgin Mary). "Pietistic make-believe"[4] has been suggested as one reason; it has been argued that perhaps a Neo-Platonic convert wanted to bring the Christian doctrines closer to his former companions by putting them into the mouth of a cultivated Athenian who had been converted by Paul.[5] There are, too, harsher critics who speak bluntly of "dubious character"[6] and "fraud."[7] "In order to secure prestige and authority, he makes himself out a disciple of the Apostle."[8]

Whatever the truth of the matter may be, the writings handed down under the name of Dionysius the Areopagite have exerted a tremendous, an inestimable, influence for more than a thousand years—and have done so *because* there was ascribed to them the almost canonical authority of the disciple of Paul.

It is true that the genuineness of these writings was called into question, even flatly contested, almost as soon as they appeared. During a theological disputation in Constantinople around 532 Bishop Hypatius of Ephesus rejected their authority and maintained that citing them proved nothing. He argued that if Dionysius the Areopagite, the disciple of Paul, had really been their author,

Athanasius and Cyril of Alexandria would certainly have known and quoted them.

But strangely enough, this mistrust soon subsided. Gregory the Great (died 604) no longer had the slightest doubts; and only a few decades later the great Greek theologian Maximus the Confessor (died 662) wrote the first commentaries. He was the first of a succession of commentators over the centuries whose distinguished company included Albertus Magnus and Thomas Aquinas. Albert, who wrote commentaries on all the Areopagite writings, held the opinion that the Holy Spirit Himself was their true author.[9] And Thomas mentions that Dionysius was said to have recorded the visions of his teacher Paul.[10] The writings of this unknown were venerated "almost like the Bible itself."[11] Evelyn Underhill[12] says that the influence of St. Augustine upon later mysticism is admittedly very great, but that it amounted to "nothing compared to that remarkable nameless personality who was pleased to ascribe his works to Dionysius the Areopagite, the friend of St. Paul." As soon, for example, as the *Mystic Theology* was translated into English, it is said, in the words of an old writer, to have coursed through England "like a swift deer."[13]

In the Latin West, and especially in France, added weight was lent to the authority of Dionysius, and once more upon the basis of an erroneous identification. In the year 827 Michael, the Byzantine Emperor, sent a copy of the Areopagite's writings to Louis the Pious. Louis thereupon asked the Abbot of Saint-Denis, one Hilduin, a pupil of Alcuin's, to collect all available information concerning Dionysius, the martyred Bishop of Paris (of the third century) who had given his name to the monastery of Saint-Denis and who lay buried in its crypt.[14]

Hilduin, who also appears to have been the first translator of the Areopagite writings, thereupon wrote his *Vita Dionysii*. In this biography he confounded the Bishop of Paris with the disciple of St. Paul, and both with the author of the books received from Byzantium. By the thirteenth century the divines at the University of Paris ranked Dionysius the Areopagite as one of the great teachers of Christianity,[15] still on the basis of the original confusion. St. Francis de Sales, a contemporary of Descartes, was still to praise the author of *On the Divine Names* as the "great apostle of France."[16]

Whether, however, we speak of naïve mistakes, of more or less pious frauds, of the cunning of the World Spirit, or of a decree of Providence, there can be no denying that the influence of the Areopagite writings preserved in the Latin West an element in the interpretation of reality which otherwise would probably have been repressed and lost for the reason that it cannot easily be co-ordinated with rationality. It is an Eastern element which in this way remained present and effective in the Occident. After the Great Schism which erected a wall between East and West that lasted for centuries, there was only one among all the great Greco-Byzantine writers who nevertheless penetrated into the schools of Western Christianity[17]: Dionysius the Areopagite. It has even been said that through translations and commentaries he himself became a Westerner "by adoption."[18]

That is an exaggeration which need not be taken too literally. For much as the Western mind needed the fruitful perturbation and the corrective of the Areopagite ferment, that Western mind was basically of another hue. And very soon, indeed, Western Christianity began to defend itself against the potential peril of being "over-whelmed by alien influences."

At this point a word must be said concerning the work of John the Scot,[19] one of the most remarkable figures in the history of medieval philosophy, whose educational influence ranks with that of Alcuin in the last quarter of the eighth century. Shortly before the year 860 this Irishman (Scot was the usual name for the Irish in the Middle Ages) translated all the Areopagite writings into Latin.[20] Four hundred years later Thomas Aquinas was to use this translation as the basis for his commentary. But John the Scot was more than a translator. He took up the thought of Dionysius the Areopagite with passionate intensity, and developed it on his own. The result was a conception of the universe which has been called "the first metaphysical synthesis of the Middle Ages."[21] The very title of John the Scot's principal work shows that this thinker was aiming to comprehend the whole "structure of nature" (*De divisione naturae*). Of this book Gilson[22] says that it momentarily offered the Latin West the opportunity and even the temptation to choose the way of the East once and for all, that way marked out by Dionysius the Areopagite and Maximus Confessor. Had that happened, the Middle Ages would have acquired a totally different aspect. But this opportunity or temptation was rejected; the Church condemned the book, chiefly for its closeness to pantheism. Nevertheless the work of John the Scot seems to have exerted a hidden but considerable influence within Western Christianity from century to century.[23]

These writings of Dionysius the Areopagite, taken up with such great eagerness, influenced the West in the most various ways. Inevitably, the extremely rational and "Western" idea of *ordo* was reinforced, deepened, and extended by the basic Areopagite tenet of "hierarchy." For "hierarchy" means: order of rank within a community comprehending all living beings and based upon divine rule. Here, however, "order" is conceived less as a static fact than as a dynamic action which must ever and again be accomplished in the life of the spirit.[24]

Through Dionysius the Areopagite the proto-Platonic idea of the *stages* in the climb to perfection found its way into Occidental spirituality. It acquired a place and a force which it was never again to lose. "Purification—Illumination—Union"—the great Spanish mystics of the sixteenth century, Theresa of Ávila and John of the Cross, were to employ these Areopagite terms to describe man's spiritual development.

Here, however, we wish to explain what sort of counterpoise the works of Dionysius Areopagiticus brought to medieval scholasticism. That element may best be summarized by the concise motto: *"negative theology and philosophy."*

Dionysius' most important work deals with the names we can apply to God. In despite of all purely rational speculation it maintains the decidedly Biblical thesis that we cannot give God any appropriate name at all, unless He himself reveals it to us. Then Dionysius proceeds to show that even the revealed names cannot possibly express the nature of God, in so far as they have to be comprehensible to our finite intellects. Certainly it is meaningful to call God "just." However, this affirmative statement requires at once the corrective of the co-ordinate negation. Our notion of "justice" derives from the empirical world, which is alone accessible to us, and in which the just man fulfills his obligations toward others with whom he has dealings: for this is the nature of justice. But it pertains to the nature of God that He has obligations toward no one. Thus it makes good sense to say: God's justice is necessarily so "different" that it cannot strictly be called justice at all. To be exact, we cannot even call God "being" and "real,"[25] since we derive these concepts from things to which God has given reality; the Creator cannot possibly be of the same nature as what He has created.[26]

Yet even definitions comprising such negations cannot cover or comprehend the nature of God. The *Mystic Theology* concludes by finally negating the negation on the ground that God infinitely surpasses anything that man may possibly say of him, whether it be affirmative or negative.

Incidentally, it would be quite inaccurate to call this fundamental corrective of all possible rationalism "irrational." To do so would be to falsify the situation; for the basis of these "negative" statements is not an unsubstantiated vague feeling, but the clear, "rational" insight that God infinitely exceeds the scope of human understanding.

Scholasticism might have learned all this from Augustine, too. *Si comprehendis, non est Deus:* "Whatever you understand cannot be God"—simply because you understand it. This is a thought that crops up many times[27] in the works of Augustine. But probably an authority of greater weight even than Augustine was needed to counteract a *ratio* discovering its own powers—and this authority was falsely attributed to the *Corpus Areopagiticum*. And in fact these writings exerted an unexpected hold over scholasticism, which had begun under such entirely different auspices.

In Thomas Aquinas, for example, there are more than seventeen hundred quotations from Dionysius the Areopagite, in addition to the commentary on the book *On the Divine Names* which Thomas wrote in the last decade of his life.[28] Now it is certainly a sign of the "universal teacher's" peculiar greatness that he vigorously incorporated into his own thinking the "unscholastic" element of negative theology and philosophy, as a counterpoise to *ratio*'s tendency to overemphasize the positive. Certainly Thomas is being entirely himself when in the *Summa Theologica* he would have the "beginner" standing on the threshold of theology[29] accept such a sentence as this: "Because we do not know what God is, but only what he is *not,* we cannot consider how he is, but only how he is *not.*" Still it is a noteworthy fact that Thomas chooses to appeal expressly to the authority of Dionysius the Areopagite whenever he speaks, as he does often, and in remarkably strong terms, of the inaccessible darkness of the ground of reality. Three such sentences, each accompanied by a formal reference to the Areopagite, will be cited here. They stand for a multitude. Oddly enough, two of them are found in Thomas' commentary on the distinctly "Aristotelian" tractate of Boethius on the Trinity.

The first sentence is: "God is honored by silence—not because we cannot say or understand anything about Him, but because we know that we are incapable of comprehending Him."[30] The second: "It is therefore said of us that when we come to the end of our knowledge, we acknowledge God as the Unknown, because the mind has made most progress in understanding when it recognizes that God's essence lies beyond anything that the mind in its state of being-on-the-way can comprehend."[31] The pithy third sentence, from the *Quaestiones disputatae*,[32] is probably the most radical "negative" formulation to be found at all in the works of St. Thomas. And we must not, incidentally, deceive ourselves about it; the validity of this sentence, as of the two previous ones, is not restricted to the realm of theology. Inevitably the sentences concern (and perhaps change) human reason's self-judgment and man's relationship to the universe in general. Certainly that is how Thomas must have meant the following statement: "This is the extreme of human knowledge of God: to know that we do not know God." In all three cases, as we have said, Dionysius the Areopagite is expressly named.[33] These sentences are replies to the challenge he laid down.

But Thomas Aquinas is mentioned here only as an example, although a most telling example. Whenever in medieval philosophy we find talk of the darkness which encloses the bright framework of dialectic reason, we may guess that the Areopagite is hovering in the wings. At the very end of the scholastic era he emerges once more in all distinctness: in the work of Nicholas of Cusa. In the library at Bernkastel Cues there remain to this day several translations of the Areopagite writings, replete, moreover, with marginal notes in the Cardinal's handwriting.[34] But even apart from this concrete evidence, it would be plain as day that Cusanus' doctrine of "knowing non-knowing" is linked to Dionysius the Areopagite's conviction that all reality is unfathomable, is indeed a mystery in the strict sense of the word.

IV

If there was any philosophical and theological thinker of importance during the Middle Ages who remained untouched by the spirit of Dionysius the Areopagite, he was *Anselm of Canterbury*. It is of course inconceivable that this highly cultivated Benedictine did not know the Areopagite writings, for they had long since become common property. But in his entire body of work the name of Dionysius is mentioned exactly once.[1] And this mention is purely factual and explanatory; it is in no way a tribute to the Areopagite. Of itself, of course, this is merely an item in literary history, and need not concern us further. But it tells us something about Anselm's peculiar contribution: Anselm's thinking dispensed with that corrective which, we have said, was embodied in Dionysius the Areopagite's "negative" theology. Hence Anselm's "practically unlimited confidence" (in Gilson's phrase[2]) in the power of reason to illuminate even the mysteries of Christian faith. Anselm was troubled by no self-critical doubts of reason.

Of course a theologian like Anselm could never subscribe to the thesis that nothing exists which is beyond the power of human *ratio* to comprehend. He was armed against that temptation. Nevertheless, it is not in the least surprising that his thinking frequently approached such rationalism. Hardly one Christian theologian today would clear Anselm of Canterbury of this charge, for all that he was a saint and Church Father.[3] When we make this criticism, we do not necessarily mean to subtract anything from the grandeur of his ideas, formulated as they were with such passion. May it not be that the greatness of Anselm, even as philosopher and theologian, was founded in something entirely different from his declared principles? Perhaps the full significance of these principles comes to light only within the man's existential field of force. This, at any rate, is what we wish to demonstrate.

Should anyone think from the name that Anselm was an Englishman, he must be told that the later Archbishop of Canterbury had for fifteen years been prior and then for another like period abbot of the monastery of Le Bec in the valley of the lower Seine. Thus he can justly be called a French Benedictine. However, his native land was not France but Italy. A Savoyard, he was born at Aosta in 1033, the son of a Lombard nobleman.

We know a good deal about the rather colorful life-story of Anselm thanks to the biography of him written by his disciple and friend, the monk Eadmer.

The biography begins with Anselm's turning his back upon his parental home, crossing the Alps to Burgundy (which in the year of his birth had been united with the German Empire), and finally reaching the Benedictine abbey of Le Bec in Normandy—attracted by the fame of its learned prior, Lanfranc. Incidentally, Lanfranc too was a Lombard, born in Pavia; and the way that lay behind him had already been as adventurous as that which the future held in store for him. Lanfranc had one of those dramatic careers which are not infrequent in the history of medieval philosophy. Schooled in Greek, he was originally a teacher of law and specialist in administration in his native city of Pavia. After some time he turned toward the *artes liberales*. In a certain sense that meant philosophy. Pupils streamed from great distances to sit at his feet. Then one day, while travelling in northern France, he was attacked, robbed, and left lying bound. He was found and released—and promptly "took leave of the world," perhaps because of a vow he had taken. He entered the nearby abbey of Le Bec as a monk.

French maps today designate the place with the double name of Le Bec-Hellouin. The addition is the name of the abbey's founder, and there is a kind of "saga" surrounding him as well; it can be quickly summarized, however. Hellouin (Herluin), a Norman knight, turned his estate into a monastery overnight. He himself later became its abbot. He had not yet learned to read and write, but such were his insights into the spiritual life that when he bared them to the distinguished novice Lanfranc, the learned man was greatly amazed.[4]

When Lanfranc in his turn became its prior, the abbey of Le Bec grew to be one of the most famous schools in Western Europe. So great was the reputation of Lanfranc that Anselm felt even deterred from entering this abbey on that account. Eadmer[5] relates that Anselm had said to himself: Cluny was obviously not the place for him, since knowledge was despised there; but if he went to Le Bec it would not be very pleasant to be constantly put in the shade by Lanfranc; Anselm thought he needed a place "where I can show my knowledge and can be helpful to a multitude." Of course the biographer hastens to say that the saintly Anselm, whenever he spoke of these matters in later days, always added: "I did not then realize what a bad thing I was saying allegedly out of love of neighbor."[6]

As it turned out, Lanfranc did not long remain in young Anselm's way. The Norman dukes embarked on the conquest of England and began the program of installing Frenchmen into the highest English offices; for almost three hundred years to come the ruling class of

England was to be French-speaking. William the Conqueror assured himself of the support of the learned jurist Lanfranc by making him Archbishop of Canterbury.

Meanwhile Anselm became the shining light of Le Bec, and his influence radiated in all directions. No less than one hundred and eighty monks entered the monastery during the fifteen years of Anselm's abbacy. "Almost all of you have come to Le Bec on my account, but none of you has become a monk on my account," he himself wrote in his farewell letter[7] to his community. For at the age of sixty he in turn had to leave because he was called to succeed Lanfranc in the Archbishop's seat at Canterbury.

But that is a euphemistic description of the actual violent events. What happened was that Anselm, visiting England on affairs of his abbey, was forced to take the office against his declared will. His hand was opened with physical force, the bishop's staff placed in it, and he was carried into the church amid singing of the *Te Deum*, protesting all the while that this "election" was invalid. Nevertheless, so it was and so it remained—all the more so since there was general sentiment among other bishops that he should be Lanfranc's successor. And now there followed fifteen years of a wearing struggle between the primate of England and the Norman kings.

After four years in office Anselm set out on a journey to Rome. The trip began under shameful circumstances: the King had the whole ship searched at Dover. Bags and wallets were brought forth and untied; as Eadmer tells it, "all the baggage was rummaged through for money."[8] Anselm wrote to the Pope: "It is well known to many persons, Holy Father, that by violence, very much against my will and despite my protestations, I was captured for the Bishop's seat in England and have been held captive there; everyone also knows how fervently I urged upon the people that my nature, my age, my weakness, my ignorance, were all entirely unsuitable to this office. . . . Now I have been Archbishop for four years—and have achieved nothing. I have lived uselessly, in fearful and unspeakable confusion of the spirit, so that every day I wish that I might rather die far from England than continue to live there."[9]

This lament is sounded again and again through the last years of Anselm's life. Eadmer recounts: "God is my witness: I have often heard him say he would rather be a boy in the abbey trembling under the teacher's rod than occupy the pastoral office of primate of all England, and take the seat of Archbishop in the assemblages of the people."[10] Occasionally this personal grief makes its way even into the pure thought of his theological treatises. Thus he takes occasion to say, in the preface to *Cur Deus homo*, that he began to write this book in England "in great affliction of heart; whence and why it has come to me—God knows."

It would be quite wrong, incidentally, to take this lament for mere self-pity on the part of a man who did not feel up to the demands of his office. In reality Anselm displayed great personal courage in opposing the King, and his activity brought lasting benefits to the Church in England. Eadmer[11] records a conversation in which Anselm replied to the King, who had spoken with extreme vehemence, in these words: "You are the master; what you will, you say. But I know for what I have been chosen and what task I have assumed in England. I must reply that it would ill comfort me to omit for the sake of transitory advantages those things which in times to come will be useful to the Church, thanks to divine mercy."

The burdens of office were never to be lifted from Anselm. He died in England, still Archbishop of Canterbury, in the year 1109, at the age of seventy-five.

We have two famous phrases coined by Anselm whereby he expressed again, in his own precise fashion, the principle of the conjunction of faith and reason which had been formulated more than five hundred years earlier by Boethius. These are: *fides quaerens intellectum* and *credo ut intelligam*. This first motto, which concerns the believer's search for understanding of what he believes, is a summation of the content of the *Proslogion*,[12] one of Anselm's most important writings; indeed, the phrase was originally intended as the title of the *Proslogion*. The second motto concludes the first chapter of the same work. Incidentally, the phrase *credo ut intelligam*, so concise as almost to invite erroneous application, may be found in almost the selfsame form in Augustine[13]; just as the idea of Boethius is likewise to be encountered in the works of Augustine—as Thomas[14] was to point out.

Anselm himself expressly refers to Augustine many times, in fact quotes him almost exclusively. It has even been said[15] that it was only through Anselm's vigorous and independent adaptations that Augustine once again became a living and effective force, after centuries during which he was sterilely quoted and copied. To be sure, Anselm's interpretation emphasized a very special aspect of Augustine. That aspect exists, without a doubt; but it is only a part of a broader spectrum: the aspect, namely, under which Augustine too appears chiefly as a "representative of *ratio*."[16]

In the preface to the *Monologion*, a small tractate which—*nota bene*—deals, among other things, with the divine Trinity, he makes two statements, one hard upon the other, which disclose the essence of his thought. He first sets forth his intention, which he says is at the express request of his brother monks, *not* to base the following argument upon the Holy Scriptures, but solely upon reason. He then confidently expresses his conviction that the tractate contains nothing which could not be harmonized with the doctrines of Augustine. Here we have what is, to my mind, the special position of Anselm.

To simplify somewhat, human reason may be overvalued in two different ways: one way is the overvaluation of experience; the other is the overvaluation of logical deduction from general principles. Of these two ways, the second seems especially linked to the Platonic-Augustinian view of the world; it is a latent peril of that view. And it is this peril of "deductive rationalism" which Anselm of Canterbury conjured up, and which thereafter lingered in Western Christianity.

The disastrous consequences of that approach—which in Anselm's day still lay in the future—have since come so fully to light that we today feel profound uneasiness, not to say alarm, when we read the rational arguments that Anselm considers sufficient proof of the truths of Christian faith. For example, Anselm attempts to demonstrate that salvation through God incarnate was necessary on compelling rational grounds. In so doing he expressly argues "without prejudice" and without reference to history, on an "as if" basis: "as if nothing were known of Christ," and "as if He had never existed."[17] Or Anselm affirms that in the Heavenly Kingdom human beings must "necessarily" take the place of the fallen angels "*because* there exist no other natures from which their number could be replaced."[18] "It can be asserted without any doubt that God incarnate had to be born of a virgin."[19] "It is necessary that the Divine Word and man unite in One Person."[20] And so on. Gilson[21] says, summing up: "St. Anselm did not shrink from the task of proving the necessity of the Trinity and the Incarnation." It is therefore not surprising that scholasticism in general became identified with the (vain) effort to make the doctrines of faith acceptable to reason, "to demonstrate by simple ratiocination what was believed," as Hegel[22] remarks in reference to Anselm.

But the matter is in fact rather complicated; and the time has come to consider this.

In the first place we may assume that rational argumentation could only show its real strength by "experiment," that is, by its actually going through and testing all the possibilities that offered. On these grounds Anselm's approach may have been a necessary first step from which ultimately Thomas' balanced view would later be developed: that necessary reasons cannot demonstrate the tenets held by faith, but can show that they are not contrary to reason[23]; and that such a use of the wisdom of the world is not a mixing of the wine (of theology) with the water (of reason), but should rather be called a changing of water into wine.[24]

Secondly, we must also recognize that Anselm's intrepid experiment was in part intended as polemic against tradition. To understand how this is so, we must know, for example, how previous theology dealt with the question of God's Incarnation. This will cast light on what was new in Anselm's line of argument and show us to what extent he was an innovator. The interpretation customary up to the time of Gregory the Great went about as follows: From the time that Adam committed the first human sin, Satan had a legal claim upon all of humanity; this claim could lose its validity and be made ineffective only by Satan's wrongfully attempting—perhaps even because he had been inveigled into the attempt—to profane an utterly sinless man, that is to say, Christ.[25] And so on. Only against this background can we see Anselm's arguments in full and distinct outline. What Anselm says is this: If man's original sin is to be extinguished in such a manner that it is not simply forgotten, but really "redeemed," paid for and "settled"—which means, in such manner that the dignity of both creditor and debtor is respected—then someone must "pay" the debt who is both at once: God and man. That is Anselm's interpretation, which has ever since been part and parcel of theology. A present-day Christian could no longer consider the earlier interpretation even as an abstract possibility.

(For the non-Christian, incidentally, and perhaps not for him alone, we must sound a cautionary note concerning the "claims to validity" of such interpretations in general. For at first glance it does seem that the "Christian point of view" is contained within these interpretations and "theories," and that consequently the content of that "Christian point of view" is always *changing*. To this, we must answer with a firm "No." The Christian's faith has to do primarily with facts, not with the interpretation of facts. The Christian believes in something real, not in this or that theory about the reality. He believes in what was revealed in the words of God; but he does not actually believe in theology. Now every interpretation, including Anselm's, is theology. What then is the believed truth which lies behind these theologies? Answer: That in the beginning something was lost to man as a punishment for a transgression; and that through the sacrifice of God incarnate, man was liberated at once from the condition of transgression and of loss. This has always been the content of the "Christian point of view" and this has never changed.)

There is a third consideration which must be mentioned in Anselm's favor. His "practically unlimited" trust in reason's powers of illumination is based, first and foremost, on faith. We need only open the *Proslogion*[26]: "I do not seek the insight of reason in order to believe; but I believe in order to gain insight; indeed, I also believe this: that I should never be able to attain insight if I did not believe." Moreover, Anselm also testified to the truths of faith being mysteries: "Whatever a man may be able to say about this [the Incarnation]—he must know that so great a thing has its deeper reasons which are still hidden from him."[27] Thus Anselm qualified his confidence in reason.

We may, to be sure, find Anselm treading on dangerous ground only a little distance from this last quotation. For we find that he claims certainty only in the sense "that for the present [*interim*] it seems so to me until God in some way should give me better revelation."[28] Here Anselm is giving himself away; far from deferring to mystery, he has said that *ratio* does not capitulate to mystery, but only to clearer understanding, that is, to the stronger argument. Only until that understanding is vouchsafed him, "for the present," meanwhile, in the interim, does it hold to its conclusions on mere faith. In passages such as these we see to what extent Anselm's real energies were directed toward the positive aspects of rational argumentation. In the abstract he could recognize reason's necessary inadequacy to cope with mystery; he acknowledged that inadequacy rationally. But he was unable to grasp it in any real sense, that is existentially.

Nevertheless both elements, *fides* and *ratio,* were conjoined within the forthright, unbending personality of Anselm, though conjoined in a highly special manner. This conjunction was accomplished not so much through any clear intellectual co-ordination of the elements as through the religious energy of this unusual and saintly man. Intellectually speaking, the conjunction was an act of violence which could not possibly last. The corrective element was contained within Anselm's personality and was therefore a chance factor. As soon as anyone else attempted to use Anselm's position as a base for further thought, the conjunction could no longer be maintained because it was conceived from the point of view of only one of the elements—which was contrary to the nature and dignity of both elements. The conjunction was bound to break up, with emphasis falling either on some kind of rationalism or on a hazardous irrationalization of faith.

In the early Middle Ages this dichotomy had not yet taken place, though some prefigurings of it could perhaps already be sensed. Thus, it could be read in the fate of the curious argument known in the history of philosophy as the "Anselmic argument." Kant would speak of it as the "ontological proof of God"[29]; but he would mention the name of Descartes rather than Anselm—a fact which suggests the further course the idea was to take.

Anselm set forth this argument in the above-mentioned *Proslogion,* which he wrote at about the age of forty-five, when he was still prior of Le Bec. When we learn from Eadmer, and Anselm himself, something of the state of mind in which the tractate was written, we are in a better position to appreciate the intellectual intensity within its pages. Eadmer[30] relates that during this period Anselm could not think of sleep, nor of eating and drinking, and that this mental fever invaded even his prayers during the canonical hours. Anselm himself reports in the foreword to the *Proslogion* that after completing his earlier treatise, *Monologion,* that "example of a consideration of the reasons for belief,"[31] he had asked himself "whether it might not be possible to discover an argument that needed no further proof outside of itself and that therefore would *alone* be sufficient to prove both the existence of God and also that He is the highest good, needing nothing but needed by all in order to be and be good. I frequently pondered hard over this matter. Sometimes I thought I already held in my grasp what I was thinking, but then it again entirely escaped the reach of my mind. Finally I wished to abandon this whole undertaking as hopeless, for it seemed to me impossible to attain my goal. But when I attempted to drive these thoughts out of my head . . . they assailed me all the more tempestuously the more I did not want them and tried to fend them off. One day, when I had already grown weary of resistance, there came to me in the midst of the conflicting thoughts exactly what I had already given up hope of ever reaching. . . . [Eadmer writes: "At night, while he lay sleepless, it was vouchsafed to him: the goal of his search appeared plainly before his mind, and his spirit was filled with immeasurable rejoicing."[32]] I think that many a reader will take pleasure in an account of this discovery, which gives me great joy, and therefore I have written the present little book."

As soon as this book, the *Proslogion,* became widely known, there began disputations on Anselm's "discovery." A polemic against it was written by a monk named Gaunilon.[33] This bore the wittily challenging title, *Answer for the Fool*—the fool, namely, being he of whom it is said in Scripture: "The fool has said in his heart, there is no God" (Ps. 13, 1). According to Gaunilon, Anselm's argument was scarcely adequate to defeat a fool of this sort. To this Anselm replied elegantly, if somewhat obliquely, in a new opusculum[34]: "Since the objection comes not from that fool . . . but one who is not a fool, rather a Catholic Christian,[35] it should suffice to reply to the Christian." The discussion, to which later Thomas Aquinas, Descartes, Leibnitz, Kant, Hegel, and many others were to add their voices, is in progress to this day. One of the last important contributions to it dates from the year 1931 and was written by Karl Barth.[36]

What, then, is the argument which was supposed to be sufficient in itself to prove the existence of God? Reduced to its concise terms, it may be rendered thus: God is that being than which nothing greater can be conceived—and therefore God must exist. For He would not be that being than which nothing greater can be conceived if He lacked existence. In short, God must exist because existence belongs to the concept of God.

This reasoning evokes a curious reaction from the average person, when he first encounters it. He feels that, despite the extreme keenness of the formal argument, there is something here which does not hold water. It is this ambiguous aspect of the argument which has kept the discussion alive up to the present.

Let us follow the steps of Anselm's syllogism somewhat more closely and see if that does not improve our understanding of the matter.

First step: What do we mean by "God" but the absolutely highest being? Everyone, including the "fool," must grant this. The superlative makes sense only if no higher being exists, even as a conceptual possibility.

Second step[37]: That which someone thinks "exists" in his thought. The state of being known or thought involves "being."

Third step: That than which nothing greater can be conceived cannot exist in thought alone; it must necessarily exist also in objective reality.

This last step calls for some examination. Let us look at the following alternatives[38]: Certainly it is possible to conceive something which nevertheless cannot exist— which would mean that such "being in thought" cannot correspond to objective existence. For example: a circular square.[39] Furthermore, there are conceivable things which although they are in fact not encountered in objective reality could possibly exist, from a purely logical point of view. For example: a winged horse like Pegasus. A third possibility: something may "be in thought" and be also in inexistence in objective reality; it could also be thought that these known and actually existing things do *not* exist. For example: all the things that we encounter in experience. Finally: something is thought which not only actually exists, but necessarily exists, so that its nonexistence cannot be conceived. The example of this, says Anselm, is God.

The force of the argument rests upon God's in fact representing a unique and incomparable case of Being itself.[40] This is a point which Anselm's first adversary, the monk Gaunilon, had missed. After all, Gaunilon said, we can certainly conceive a "Blessed Isle," brimming with riches and joys of every kind, lost in the illimitable ocean; and naturally we will "understand" and "know" very well what this idea is all about. But, Gaunilon continued, suppose someone were to tell me about such an isle, and finish by saying, as though this necessarily followed from

68

his account, that this isle which had no match in all the world *must* really exist. "For you cannot deny that it 'exists' in your thoughts; but since it is the most superb island that can possibly be imagined, it cannot possibly exist only in your thoughts; it must also "be" in reality; for otherwise every really existing island would be superior to it. Suppose, I say, someone were to attempt to prove by such devices that that isle must be in actual existence, and that there could no longer be any doubt of it, I should either think he had been joking, or I should not know whom to think the more foolish: myself if I were to believe such a thing, or him if he thought he had proved anything in such a way."

However, this hearty, clear, sound, and also irrefutable argument does not meet Anselm's idea head-on. Hegel perceived that quite correctly when he said of Kant's counterargument that it missed the point. Gaunilon, Hegel says,[41] criticized Anselm's argument in the same inadequate fashion "as Kant has in the present day: on the ground that being and thought are different. Thus Kant, for example, says: If we imagine 100 taler, this imagining does not include their existence. And that is correct. . . . But it is also no novelty at all that they are different; Anselm knew this every bit as well as Kant." So much for Hegel.

Anselm's line of argument rests upon the fact that the nature of the existence of God is different in principle from the nature of all other existences, such as that of the island or of the hundred taler. "The conclusion, 'God exists,' occupies a special position."[42] We cannot make exact analogies between God and any other phenomenon, for to exist actually belongs to the essence of God. This observation, however, I hasten to add, is not in itself identical with the premise, "God exists." Evidently, from the foregoing demonstration, it is just as difficult to refute Anselm's line of argument as to suppress the suspicion that there is something fundamentally wrong about it.

Of late various people have come forth in support of Anselm on grounds which, strangely enough, were never urged during the Middle Ages. Thus, it is maintained that Anselm's argument has nothing whatsoever to do with a "proof of God." "Anselm had not the slightest intention of proving the existence of God," says one modern member of Anselm's order.[43] Indeed, he continues, Anselm's idea not only had nothing to do with philosophy, but also nothing to do with theology in the sense of a disputatious science; rather, the *Proslogion* was "an essay in *mystical* theology."[44] There are other interpretators—all within our own time—who take a similar view.[45] Chief of these is Karl Barth, who writes: "It [Anselm's argument] was not a question of a science departing from the faith of the Church and attempting to found the faith of the Church upon a source *outside* itself. It was a question of theology. It was a question of proof of the faith which even beforehand and without proof was firm in itself through faith. . . . Time and again, various persons have dubbed Anselm's proof of the existence of God the 'ontological' proof. . . . That represents a carelessness in thinking, and is an error upon which we need waste no further words."[46]

In line with this interpretation these writers point out, for example, that the argument of Anselm's *Proslogion* only gives the appearance of being purely rational, for it is enclosed within a prayer with which the argument begins and ends. This is certainly so, and such a prayer seems inappropriate for a work which purports to be scientific. A scientific work cannot thus assume what is to be proved. Yet there is no gainsaying the fact that Anselm himself speaks of wishing to provide so conclusive a proof that it will "need no other outside of itself"[47]; he makes the statement that he does *not* want to base this proof on Holy Scripture; and even in the prayer which winds up the argument[48] he says: "Even if I did not want to *believe* in Thy Existence, I would now [which can only mean: on the basis of my argument] be incapable of not *acknowledging* Thee." But this is the most telling evidence: that Anselm obviously did not feel that he had been misunderstood when Gaunilon took the *Proslogion* to be a rational line of argument which he tried to refute with exclusively rational counterarguments. And indeed, the same procedure was to be followed throughout the rest of the Middle Ages. On the basis of rational arguments Bonaventura would agree; and likewise on the basis of such arguments Thomas would refuse to agree.

To be sure, Descartes would also accept the Anselmic reasoning. Yet it becomes evident that Anselm after all meant something quite different from Descartes. In that regard Karl Barth is most convincing; we must concur when he says that Anselm's argument "is on a different plane from the well-known doctrine of Descartes and Leibnitz," and that it is "not remotely affected" by "what arguments Kant has advanced against these doctrines."[49] Nevertheless, it is significant that Descartes could imagine he was saying the same thing as Anselm.

Descartes put the thing in various ways.[50] The clearest of his formulations is this: "I saw very well that if a triangle is assumed, its three angles must equal two right angles. But I did not yet see that this included any proof that a triangle must exist in the world—whereas when I considered the idea of a perfect being . . . I found that existence is just as inherent to this idea as it was inherent to the idea of a triangle that its three angles should equal two right angles; indeed, it is even more so. Consequently, the statement that God, as this perfect being, is, or exists, is at least quite as incontrovertible as any geometrical proof can be."[51] We can say with a fair degree of certainty that Anselm would scarcely have recognized his own argument had he encountered it in the context of Descartes's *Discours de la méthode*. But where lies the difference? The difference is that the *Discours* attempts to be "pure" philosophy and that Descartes's line of argument has been preceded by a deliberate severance from the concept of God held by faith. Given Anselm's starting point—to wit, his overvaluation of deductive reason—that severance is not altogether unexpected. In fact, it was actually inevitable.

The attempt to fuse faith and reason, which began with Boethius and for the first time was put consistently and radically into practice by Anselm's passion for rationality, can probably never lead to a lasting result, to a "solution" valid for all time. At any rate, it never has done so. When, on the one hand, it acknowledges a superhuman standard of truth, and, on the other hand, attempts to assimilate the growing body of critical knowledge of the universe and man, speculative reason necessarily flirts with instability. Seeking such a double end, it makes things difficult for itself—inevitably, for wisdom is not a facile thing. Under these conditions speculative reason will forever be running risks. It may either be tempted to overestimate its own powers, or it may resign itself to agnosticism. It may go astray into slavish devotion to science, into deductive or empirical rationalism; or it may retreat into traditionalism and fideism; and so forth.

Assuming, then, that probably no final solution is possible, let us for a moment consider the way in which Thomas Aquinas met the challenge of Anselm's argument.

Thomas' answer, it seems to me, actually achieves a linking of the two elements, and not only by way of a balance of stresses within the mind of the thinker himself. It also achieves an intellectual balance based upon an intelligent distribution of the weights to be given to faith and reason. Nevertheless, however Thomas puts it, we sense that the question was fraught with strong emotion, for this was a discussion which had been waged for more than two centuries, by the time Thomas attempted to deal with it. Then again, Thomas' answer—so careful in its distinctions, so entirely non-"radical," and formulated with such extreme alertness to its every implication —terrifyingly reveals Descartes's monstrous simplification of the subject.

Thomas examined Anselm's argument many times.[52] In the *Quaestiones disputatae de veritate*[53] his initial question is this: Is the fact that God exists known to the human mind of itself, just as the first principles of thought whose nonvalidity cannot even be thought, are known of themselves? Thomas first offers the historical observation that there are three different opinions regarding this matter. The *first:* That God exists cannot be proved, nor is it known of itself; it can only be believed. The *second* opinion: It is not known of itself that God exists, but it can be proved—"proved" meaning here demonstrating something not immediately known by means of something immediately known. *Third:* "Others, *such as Anselm,* are of the opinion that God's existence is known of itself, since no one can within himself think that God is not—even though he may say so outwardly and even though he may inwardly think the words in which he says it."

Of these three historical opinions, Thomas concludes that the first is obviously false. The other two, he says, are true in a certain sense. The decisive question, of course, is how we are to understand the concept "known of itself." And in considering this point, Thomas makes a distinction which enables him also to distinguish true from false in Anselm's argument. His reasoning is as follows: "Known of itself" is a proposition whose predicate pertains to the idea of its subject. But this pertinence itself need not necessarily be known to everyone; it is, of course, known only to one who knows the subject. Thus on the one hand there are propositions which are in fact known to everyone: for example, the proposition that the whole is greater than any part. On the other hand there are propositions "known of themselves" which nevertheless are by no means known to everyone, but only to the expert, the "connoisseur": for example, the proposition that incorporeal beings do not require space and exist in no "place." Having established this distinction, Thomas now confronts Anselm's argument in a new way. His logic runs as follows: Because existence is necessarily contained within the concept of God, the proposition "God exists" is actually "known of itself." But for us it is nevertheless not "known of itself"—as long as we do not know the subject of the proposition, that is to say, the being of God. If, however, we come to see God's essence, "then that God exists will be far more 'known of itself' to us

74

than it is now 'known of itself' to us that Yes and No cannot both be simultaneously valid."

In other words, Thomas would turn to Anselm and say: "You speak as one who knows God's being directly, whereas I . . ." At this point a number of modern defenders of Anselm would object that this is precisely what they have been saying, that Anselm was speaking out of the experience of mystic vision, that his argument was "a piece of mystic theology."[54] Thomas might be inclined to grant this. But he would continue: ". . . Whereas I speak from the ordinary point of view of men here on earth [as, incidentally, Anselm's argument does in its actual text, at least]. And we ordinary men are so constituted that we do *not* know God directly. We have only two ways of knowing God, both indirect. The one is faith, the other rational demonstration."

Kant's objections to Descartes's "ontological proof of God" point in a similar direction. We surely do know what a triangle is, Kant says; but we do not know what God is. "And so an object which lies wholly outside the sphere of our intellect was represented as if we very well understood what was meant by the concept of it."[55] Thomas, of course, would never say that God "lies wholly outside the sphere of our intellect"; but he, too, insists that our knowledge of God must remain inadequate, and that this inadequacy is in principle insurmountable. Thus, Thomas says,[56] even the fact that we are capable of conceiving of the nonexistence of God can very well accord with God's nevertheless being that Being than which nothing greater can be conceived; and on the other hand God's existence remains "known of itself" although we, "because of the impotence of our understanding," can only derive His existence from His works.[57] "There is no

75

obstacle to the created truth being more known to us than the uncreated; for what is less known in itself is, according to the philosopher, more known to us."[58]

This last sentence, in which Thomas refers to "the philosopher"—that is to say, Aristotle—opens up a wider perspective against which the centuries-old discussion of the pros and cons of Anselm's argument can be understood. For the ceaselessness of the discussion is not due only to the counterpoint of faith and knowledge. It is also due to an opposition of two basic attitudes which cannot be reconciled in a "synthesis"—polar attitudes which we customarily sum up (greatly simplifying) under the names of "Plato" and "Aristotle." In this context Aristotle stands for the belief that man, through study of objective reality and assembling of concrete experience, can arrive by inductive reasoning at essential knowledge; whereas the name Plato stands for the alternate belief that man is so constituted that he can get at the essential reality of the world *directly*, not through the medium of external experience; that, in other words, by closing his eyes as if summoning up remembrance, man can gain entry into the heart of reality.

It is clear at first glance that the thinkers who accept Anselm's argument stand on the side of Plato—which within the framework of Occidental philosophy virtually means: on the side of Augustine. Their company includes Alexander of Hales, Bonaventura, Albertus Magnus, and Duns Scotus, as well as Descartes and Leibnitz. As for Anselm himself, in the very first sentences of the *Proslogion*[59] we come upon the key Platonic phrase: "Enter into the chamber of your heart. . . ."

V

One of our most honored clichés is that of "medieval man." To point out how stupid such conceptions can be, Gilson[1] ironically suggests that we remember "that wild little Frenchwoman" Héloïse, Abélard's lover, who as a girl of seventeen knew Latin, Greek, and Hebrew, and who entered a convent for love of Abélard, and recited verses of the Roman poet Lucan while she took the veil. Abélard himself has described it: "Amid tears and sobs she uttered the lament of Cornelia: 'Oh glorious husband, worthy of a better marital bed. Has fate been permitted to strike such a head with such weight? Ah, did I have to wed thee to become thy misfortune?—But now take my sacrifice—gladly I offer it to thee.' That was her farewell to the world. With resolute tread she stepped up to the altar, quickly took the veil consecrated by the bishop, and before the assembled community made the vow."[2] And this happened not in Medicean Florence but three hundred years earlier, around 1120, in Argenteuil, near Paris. "Before anyone may claim to have found a formula defining the Middle Ages, he must first find a definition of Héloïse."[3]

It is not surprising, then, that the same individualistic variety, which withstands any classification by "types," should obtain in medieval philosophy as well. But what we perhaps do not expect are the vast contrasts in theoretical positions also, often within the same generation— for example, among the contemporaries of Héloïse, the astonishing disparity in opinions, style of life, and destiny among such men as Peter Abélard, Bernard of Clairvaux, and John of Salisbury.

All three men knew one another. The first two were

each other's adversaries and counterpoises throughout their lives; the third was a pupil of the one and a protégé of the other. A visitor to France in the year 1140 could have met all three. In that year Abélard had already reached the end of his tempestuous career; at the age of sixty he was about to take refuge in the abbey of Cluny, where he was to spend the last year of life remaining to him. Bernard of Clairvaux, ten years his junior, was at the height of a life likewise full of vicissitudes as reformer, preacher of Crusades, writer on philosophy and theology, and simultaneously a man of mystic experiences. John of Salisbury, a scholar of twenty-five, took an attitude toward both his masters compounded of reverence and critical respect. All three were extremely representative figures of the twelfth century, and left their mark on subsequent philosophy for a long time to come. This is true even of Bernard of Clairvaux, although his thought belongs more to the realm of theology.

We happen on another surprising element in the history of medieval philosophy when we consider Abélard and Bernard: namely, how *young* these writers and *magistri* were when they began their public activity. Nothing is wider of the mark than the image of white-bearded monks sitting in cells remote from the bustle of the world and penning on parchment their tractates. Boethius was all of twenty years old when he wrote the first of his books which were to influence so many centuries to come. He began the commentaries on Aristotle at twenty-five. At thirty Anselm of Canterbury was prior in Le Bec. Bonaventura, already a university teacher at twenty-seven, was called at the age of thirty-six to be General of a Franciscan order that had already spread through the entire West. Duns Scotus wrote his principal work, the enormous *opus Oxoniense,* at the age of thirty-five. And William of Ockham was only twenty-five when he turned his back for good upon his distinguished career in science and letters.

Peter Abélard, born in Brittany in 1079, was still only a boy when he attended the famous Roscelin's school of philosophy. He was barely twenty when he went to Paris and, after two or three years of studying, himself opened a school of philosophy, at first on the outskirts of the city. At the age of twenty-nine he marked the success of his school by moving it to Paris itself, situating it in what is today the university quarter. In 1115 he was head of the cathedral school of Notre Dame—all of thirty-five years old. Shortly afterward he met Héloïse. Abélard himself relates in his autobiographical *Story of My Adversities (Historia calamitatum)* [4] how out of sensual passion rather than love he set about seducing this girl, his pupil. After she had had a child by him, they were wed in secret. Since Abélard was a cleric but not a priest, he was not forbidden to marry. Such marriages were not even uncustomary; nevertheless, it was kept secret so that people should continue to think the celebrated man "a Seneca or a St. Jerome." Gilson adds: "Abélard and Héloïse never forgot themselves, and that is what entangled them all the deeper in falsehood." [5] There followed the gruesome vengeance of Héloïse's guardian, who had Abélard beset and emasculated. The famous, self-assured professor ("I imagined I was the only philosopher in the world; I defied all attacks . . ." [6]) had to crawl off into a monastery. Saint-Denis took him in. At Abélard's request, Héloïse likewise retired from the world. And there now began that strange reversal of the relationship. Abélard, origi-

nally dominated solely by the craving for pleasure, underwent a true inner transformation, whereas Héloïse, who
from the beginning had loved with self-sacrificing devotion, obstinately laid stress upon the "earthly" character
of her love. "After all, my taking the veil was not done
out of love of God; it was done solely in obedience to
your command"; "I am more concerned to please you
than to please God"[7]; never yet had she done anything
in the convent out of love of God, and hence God owed
her no reward[8]—Héloïse's letters abound in such statements.[9] She appears to be utterly deaf to Abélard's fervent
pleas.[10] Even the characteristic salutations, poetic and
choicely expressed in their own right, reveal something of
the despairing drama of this correspondence. Persistently,
throughout the letters, we find these opposing forms of
address.[11] On the one hand: "To Héloïse, his most be-
loved sister in Christ, from Abélard, her brother in
Christ"; or, "To the bride of Christ from the servant of
Christ." And on the other hand: "To her absolute master,
from his utterly submissive servant"; or "To my master,
no, my father; to my husband, no, my brother; from his
maid, no, his daughter; his wife, no, his sister; to my
Abélard from his Héloïse."

Naturally Abélard, for his part, was not going to bury
himself in Saint-Denis forever. His passion for teaching
was too strong, and after some time he resumed his career.
Moreover, he had long since antagonized his hosts—by
denying that Dionysius the Areopagite had ever had any
connection with the abbey of Saint-Denis. Wherever
Abélard went, strife was bound to follow. There was not
a single one of his teachers with whom he had not quar-
relled, and whom he did not ridicule with mockery as
spiteful as it was epigrammatically witty. "His fire filled

the house with smoke, but gave no light. . . . A tree with an ample crown, amazing to behold at a distance; but from close up not even the sharpest eye could detect any fruit on it."[12]

At last, however, his boldness went too far, and an essay of his on the Trinity—ever since Boethius a standard subject for logical speculation—was condemned by a synod. That meant the end of his teaching in Paris. Abélard retired to solitude somewhere in the Seine valley; but within a short time his refuge became public knowledge. Students flocked to him; shelters had to be built for them. Yet only five years later Abélard was again a fugitive. From what? He himself says: from the "envy of the Franks, which I know all too well."[13] He found his way to the notorious monastery of Saint-Gildas on the Breton coast, and became its abbot. In his *Historia calamitatum* he writes: "Thus in blind terror of the menacing sword a man leaps into the abyss, running into the arms of death here in order to escape it there for a moment. . . . Face to face with the wildly roaring billows of the sea, at the very end of the earth, where there was no longer any possibility of fleeing still farther away, I often groaned in my prayers in the words of the Psalms: 'From the ends of the earth I cry to Thee, for my soul is in fear' "[14] Once again he was falling out with the monks. "In the face of their daily threats against me, I had to take the greatest possible care in eating and drinking; finally they put poison into the communion cup in order to poison me during the High Mass."[15] (If this seems too fantastic, we may note what Gilson[16] says in his study of Héloïse and Abélard: "Everything is medieval: . . . St. Thomas composing the office for Corpus Christi Day, and those clerics of Paris University who in 1276 had to be forbidden to play at dice, the while swearing by God, the Virgin, and all the saints, upon the very altar at which . . . day after day the body and blood of the Lord was celebrated. Now which of these facts is more 'medieval'?")

Abélard, it must be added, was threatened not only by outward circumstances. His inner turmoil was equally dangerous. "Satan had so entangled me in his snares that I have nought whereon I can rest or live like a man; like Cain after he had been cursed, I wander about, restive and fugitive everywhere. Incessantly I am tormented by 'strife without, fear within' [II Cor. 7, 5]—ah no, by everlasting strife *and* fear without *and* within."[17]

Seven years later he took flight again, going from Saint-Gildas to Paris to establish himself once more as a teacher of dialectic on Mount Sainte-Geneviève. During this period John of Salisbury became his pupil. He was also joined by men like *Arnold of Brescia,* who instinctively sensed his affinity with Abélard. Arnold, an extremely strict ascetic, at the same time a political agitator and demagogue and revolutionary against Emperor and Pope, was likewise a permanent fugitive or exile. Ultimately he fell into the power of Frederick Barbarossa, was hanged and burned, and his ashes strewn into the Tiber.

Abélard soon came again under sharp criticism. Bernard of Clairvaux lashed out against Abélard's "rationalism." The question at issue was still that of conjoining belief and rational knowledge, in accord with the principle of Boethius. Bernard, however, asserted[18]: "This man disputes concerning faith in order to attack faith. He sees nothing as reflection and parable; he looks at everything face to face. He goes farther than is meet for him. . . . Of all that exists in heaven and earth, he maintains, nothing is unknown to him unless it be himself. He shifts the boundary stones set by our forefathers by bringing under discussion the sublimest questions of Revelation. To his totally unseasoned students, mere beginners in theology, who have scarcely outgrown dialectics and are barely qualified to grasp the elementary truths of religion —to such he exposes the mystery of the Trinity, the inner sanctuary and the royal tabernacle. He presumes to imagine that he can entirely comprehend God by the use of his reason [*totum quod Deus est, humana ratione arbitratur se posse comprehendere*]." After another condemnation by the Church—which Bernard forced through in what appears to have been a not very honorable fashion—Abélard was sentenced to lifelong confinement to a monastery. As was his custom, he showed himself docile and obedient, but lost no time appealing to the Papal See. He was on his way to Rome when the Abbot of Cluny pressed him, with great kindness, to stay at the monastery. There at Cluny Abélard finally enjoyed peace, for the last year of his life.

Under the leadership of this abbot, *Petrus Venerabilis,* who incidentally had assumed his office at the age of twenty-eight, Cluny had greatly changed. A few generations before it had frightened off Anselm by its ascetic enmity to scholarship. Now it had become a center of learned studies. At the abbot's instance, for example, the first Latin translation of the Koran had just been made there.[19] Petrus Venerabilis was a friend of Bernard of Clairvaux as well as of Abélard, and also an admirer of the learned Héloïse, as we know from several letters. ("I was still a youth when your fame had already reached my ears. . . . You held high the banner of science; you raised yourself above all other women, and there are very few men whom you have not surpassed. . . ."[20]) Above all,

Petrus Venerabilis was one of the great peacemakers of the age. He brought about the reconciliation of Abélard with the Church, and even with Bernard of Clairvaux.

"I will put it briefly," Petrus declared in a letter[21] to Héloïse in which he described the transformation of Abélard during his last days. "His mind constantly dwelt upon the divine mystery. . . . He lived with us, simply and righteously . . . and devoted the last period of his life to the Lord." He himself took charge of the liturgy of the funeral and had Abélard buried in the convent headed by Héloïse, in accord with his wish.[22] Abbot Petrus also composed the verses for Abélard's grave, which begin with the words: "Gaul's Socrates, great Plato of Hesperia, our Aristotle . . ."[23]

We must remember this unusual biography when we ask ourselves what Abélard means for the history of philosophy. Grabmann, rarely inclined to sharp judgments, answers that question as follows: "No man of speculation, or of great metaphysical . . . perspectives; . . . a master of dialectic who delighted in the slash and parry of his wit and prided himself most on his skill in the setting up of new paradoxes."[24] Abélard said of himself: "Of all philosophy, logic most appealed to me. . . . To study logic I travelled—a wandering philosopher in the manner of antiquity—to every center of this science that I heard praised."[25]

To Abélard, however, "logic" was above all linguistic logic, "critical analysis of thought on the basis of linguistic expression."[26] In this, it is easy to see, Abélard came fairly close to modern approaches. Or consider the so-called "problem of universals." (This is the question whether there is something "outside," in objective reality, which corresponds to the phenomena of the world. Is

84

there, for example, a reality standing not only for "Socrates" or "Plato," but also for such common names as "man" or "rose"? Or do such common names ["universals"] possess only the "reality" of subjective thought or perhaps merely of the sound of the word [*flatus vocis*]?) It has been asserted that this was the principal, or even the only, subject of medieval philosophy. This is hardly so, although it is true that this question greatly occupied philosophers from the time of Boethius on.[27] Abélard went at the problem with a great deal of keenness, and quite sensibly from the viewpoint of linguistic logic.

On the other hand, for all his intellectual sharpness, Abélard's formulations had something journalistic about them. This weakness sprang from his penchant for things merely interesting, and for polemic. Naturally, his immediate effect upon his contemporaries was extraordinary, "incomparably greater" than the influence of Anselm of Canterbury—so we read in a modern handbook of medieval philosophy,[28] which, however, quickly adds that Anselm's thought is alive today whereas Abélard's remains only of historical interest.

Nevertheless there is a good deal in Abélard's work that proved fruitful for future investigations and clarifications. His name will always be enshrined in the history of logic,[29] for example. Of permanent value, too, is the sharp analysis, inspired no doubt by his personal history, of the meaning of conviction and intention for moral action. Without evil intent, he says, there is no sin; and to follow conscience is good even when conscience errs. By way of illustration he then discusses—and this is typical Abélard—such extreme cases as the guilt or innocence of the executioners of Jesus Christ.[30]

This idea, linked with a consistent affirmation of the natural reason common to all men, leads him to make a new positive evaluation of pre-Christians and non-Christians in general. The old thesis of Justin and of Clement of Alexandria recurs here, formulated more sharply and boldly: that the great sages of antiquity were at bottom Christians.[31] Thomas Aquinas would ultimately carry this thought to an even more radical conclusion, though phrasing it more temperately: that whoever, among pre-Christians and non-Christians, held the conviction that God will be in some manner best known to Himself the saviour of mankind, that man was a believer in Christ (*fide implicita*).[32] In Abélard's time, and above all in Abélard's deliberately "freethinking"[33] interpretation (he reads the Christian doctrine of the Trinity into Plato, for example[34]), such language was painful to orthodox ears. As Bernard of Clairvaux protested, by making Plato a Christian you merely show that you yourself are a pagan.[35]

Abélard's primary concern was completely legitimate. Its recurrent urgency is evident, to the present day, and its controversiality almost inevitable. That concern is to test to what extent reason can be applied to the realm of theology proper, and to discover the formal logical principles of such an undertaking. To sum up the outcome: Abélard on the one hand contributed a great deal by his penetrating analyses; on the other hand, he discredited the whole effort by his reckless delight in scoring polemical hits. His attitude toward his opponents was also at fault. Thus, he made all his fellow debaters into enemies[36]— and was convinced that they were one and all motivated by jealousy and inferiority. "I occupied myself . . . with elucidating the foundations of our Christian religion by analogies from the sphere of human reason. . . . My students . . . desired a comprehensible philosophical argument; they wanted to hear things they could understand . . . saying that one can believe only when one has understood. . . . My book found many readers and won great applause from all. . . . The readers were not niggardly in their appreciation of the subtlety of the answers to such weighty questions. . . . This mightily incensed those who envied me, and they convoked a council against me."[37] And so on.

How impossible it is to formulate a single definition for the Middle Ages, says Gilson,[38] is dramatized by the fact that the same age could contain both Abélard and Bernard of Clairvaux. In saying this, Gilson is thinking not so much of the disagreement between them as of the profound contrast between their natures.[39]

Bernard of Clairvaux is a personality whom it is extremely difficult to characterize accurately, for he was made up of apparently incompatible traits and qualities.

Born around 1090 to a Burgundian family of the nobility dwelling in the vicinity of Dijon, Bernard was given the education of future knight. At about twenty-one years of age he entered the monastery of Cîteaux, together with four of his brothers and twenty-five friends, all of them likewise young nobles. Cîteaux, founded only a decade before, had from the beginning been conceived as a "reform" monastery, directed against what had become the average trend, against the customary flouting of the original monastic ideals, which were here to be restored in their pure strictness. Among other things, Cîteaux was ranged against Cluny, which had departed from its own reformist beginnings and begun to be "humanistic." The friendly strife which lasted for years between Bernard of Clairvaux and Petrus Venerabilis had its origin in this antinomy.

Three years after his entrance into Cîteaux Bernard was sent forth to found the abbey of Clairvaux and, of course, to head it—at the age of twenty-four. Before Bernard reached the age of fifty, some seventy new abbeys were to be founded with Clairvaux as a center. And the leading spirit behind this amazingly dynamic development was Bernard. It is evident that a man of such passionate drive, such vital intensity, was not primarily concerned with purely intellectual "problems." Nevertheless, Bernard left behind a rather impressive body of literary work. In addition to sermons and mystic meditations he wrote such penetrating theoretical analyses as is contained in the tractate on free will. Above all we might call him, in a very special sense, a man of contemplation—*quel contemplante,* as Dante[40] says.

Bernard's particular peril, however, as his first biography already suggested, was *nimia nimietas,*[41] measureless immoderateness. The phrase is apt in many different senses: it applies to the merciless self-castigation which shattered his physical health; it applies also to his fierce and unremitting struggles against those who he decided were noxious vermin in the Kingdom of God—like Abélard. A kind of demonic violence came to the fore in his activities directed toward the world outside the monastery. Those activities often went far beyond spiritual matters and entered the realm of politics. Bernard once described himself with a curious phrase. He was, he said, "a kind of chimera of the century," "driven about through the abysses of the world."[42] And looking back upon his life, upon his dispute with Abélard, upon the Crusade for which he had inflamed the whole West by his preaching, and which had ended in a dreadful disaster—considering all this in retrospect, he said in a letter: "All my works frighten me, and what I do is incomprehensible to me."[43]

Bernard's role in the history of philosophy has been described as "struggle against dialectics in theology." To me, this description is unsatisfactory. For one thing, it does not sufficiently stress the positive aspects of his work. Bernard did indeed renew the warning contained in the work of Dionysius the Areopagite,[44] and gave it fresh force by marshalling new arguments and presenting the doctrine in his own aggressive manner. Nevertheless, Bernard was primarily concerned with something other than "negative theology." He was certainly not interested in the abstract problem of the methodological relationship of philosophy and theology to one another, and to the argument that the former ought to "serve" the latter. Nor can we find in Bernard a principled negation of knowledge or of philosophy. "There are many," he says,[45] "who seek knowledge for the sake of knowledge: that is curiosity. There are others who desire to know in order that they may themselves be known: that is vanity. Others seek knowledge in order to sell it: that is dishonorable. But there are also some who seek knowledge in order to edify others: that is love [caritas]. And again there are still others who seek knowledge in order to be edified: that is prudence."

On the other hand, we also find him saying: What do I care about philosophy? "My teachers are the apostles. . . . They have taught me to live. Do you think it a little thing, to know how to live?"[46] Such words, which expose his deepest attitudes, must not be taken as evidence of an aloof religiosity. Rather, they are expressive of what has been the true aim of philosophy since the days of Socrates and Plato. Plainly, Bernard's passionate and truly "philo-sophical" interest was entirely directed toward full "reali-zation," toward existential Wholeness, which is to say "salvation." And he regarded all forms of human expres-sion, his philosophizing as well as his theology, as de-signed to serve that Whole.

It was precisely this kind of salvation that Bernard considered to be endangered and undermined by "dialec-ticians" of the type of Abélard. The danger which he quite rightly saw dawning in such personalities, and which he fought with all his might, was nothing less than this: that the substance of Truth, by which living man is nourished, would be consumed by an empty for-malism of "correct" thinking—consumed and reduced to the vanishing point.

"Burning," said Bernard, had to be added to knowl-edge.[47] By the end of his life, when he had all but burned himself away, he summed up this philosophy in a succinct and memorable phrase. It is to be found in his last ser-mons on the Song of Songs[48]; there are, incidentally, more than eighty such sermons in Bernard's works. The whole thing is said in only three words: *anima quaerens Verbum*. It is a variation on Anselm's *fides quaerens intellectum*. Only he substitutes for the abstract elements of "faith" and "insight" the more concrete terms "soul" and "Word." "The soul in search of the Word." But, he explains, the Word can be found only by the going out of oneself (*ecstasis*) of mystic contemplation in which the soul "enjoys the Word." What in truth happens in that state cannot be communicated in human language: *ineffabile est*.[49] This, we may say, was the essential mes-sage of the mystic Bernard of Clairvaux.

With *John of Salisbury*, Abélard's and Bernard's younger contemporary, a totally different type of personality joins in the philosophical discourse—and one, incidentally, of unmistakably Anglo-Saxon cast. Here was an empiricist, on principle distrustful of dialectics, no matter how rigorous, and of all sweeping generalities and "syntheses" of metaphysical and theological speculation. Here was a man who relied primarily upon concrete experience and specific historical knowledge, and who would be content to keep his thought within such boundaries. He was destined to make a contribution to philosophy which, in ever-fresh variations, would henceforth remain a permanent strand in the fabric of European thought.

John of Salisbury, born between 1110 and 1120 in southern England, went to France as a young scholar. He was resolved to study everything there was to learn in the fields of philosophy and theology—and he made a special point of meeting all the best and most celebrated teachers of the time. After twelve years of study he made a significant and characteristic decision. This independent and cultivated young "gentleman" did not choose a learned profession. Instead of teaching, he became what we may call a diplomat. "With him begins the long line of English intellectuals who were simultaneously statesmen, Churchmen, humanists, philosophers, and writers."[50] Sponsored by Bernard of Clairvaux, John of Salisbury became secretary to the Primate of England, Archbishop Theobald of Canterbury. He remained in this office under Theobald's successor, Thomas Becket, whose close friend he became. Thus he was in a position to know all the twists and turns in the long struggle between the King and the Archbishop. He accompanied Becket into exile in France, and when both returned to England he was present at the assassination of the Archbishop in Canterbury Cathedral. He was as closely associated with England as with France, and constantly travelled between them. He also visited Italy five times. These journeys were connected with political missions on behalf of the Archbishop, the Pope, the King of England. A few years before his death in 1180 he was called to the episcopal seat of Chartres.

During the years of exile John of Salisbury wrote his two most important books, the *Metalogicus* and the *Policraticus*. He dedicated both books to his friend the Archbishop. They are unlike previous works of their type in that their abstract theoretical debate is constantly leavened and given force by extremely concrete description of historical reality directly experienced. The language, too, is unusual: an elegant, cosmopolitan rather than "scholastic" Latin based on Cicero—on which score John of Salisbury was to be virtually the only medieval author to find favor in the judgments of the later, antischolastic humanists.

The "inner" style of these books is possibly even more characteristically Anglo-Saxon: the calm, uncompromising, but never overzealous assurance of one who has carefully studied many things with his own eyes; and the faintly ironic humor of "understatement" which to this day remains so winning a trait of English prose. These qualities are more important than the subjects of these books, though they too are noteworthy: the *Metalogicus* deals with the right way to philosophize, while the *Policraticus* may be considered a kind of philosophical manual of political science, or an essay in political philosophy.

Of lasting pertinence was the point John wished to make when he deplored the sterile dialectical discussions dear to Parisian professors. Philosophy was doomed, he maintained, if it attempted "to live by logic alone."[51]

Dialectic "remains infertile if it is not fructified from elsewhere."[52] To be sure, John of Salisbury was equally wary of abstract discussion of general metaphysical problems; he held that such discussion could not constitute the true task of the philosophical man. Since, for example, no one could expect an unequivocal answer to the questions of the substance of the soul and its origins, the workings of Providence, or the nature of pure spirits,[53] philosophers should content themselves with practical probabilities and turn their attention to patient investigation, with the greatest possible exactitude, of concrete things. This principled distrust of the pretensions of speculative methodology occasionally sounds very like skepticism. But we cannot classify John of Salisbury as a shallow skeptic. He says neither that truth is absolutely unattainable nor that all is relative. His wariness is based on two factors. The first is a courageous recognition of the inadequacy of human powers of cognition: "All creature knowledge is limited."[54] The second factor is a religious respect for that truth which we do not grasp when we satisfy our desire for a closed philosophical system, but only when we come face to face with reality as it really is: simultaneously knowable and unfathomable.

Thus, in the position of John of Salisbury, we may see the first signs of the attitude which was to take shape in the thirteenth century in the form of a return to Aristotle: experience crying out to be heard independently of tradition and authority. Experience would be equated with the world as it was encountered in all its richness. In the thirteenth century, too, the task of conjoining faith with natural cognition would still be paramount. But the new attitude would lend a novel, richer, and also more dangerous cast to the manner in which that task was met.

93

VI

Our imaginary visitor to France, had he visited the Parisian Canons of Saint-Victor in the year 1140, would have found a German there, Count von Blankenburg, who won fame under the name of *Hugh of Saint-Victor*. A hundred years later Bonaventura[1] would rank him even above Anselm of Canterbury and Bernard of Clairvaux. Anselm, Bonaventura was to say, had been great in rational argumentation, Bernard in preaching, Richard[2] in mystic vision—but Hugh had been great in all these at one and the same time.

Born in Hartingam in the Harz Moutains in 1096, Hugh was sent to Paris at the age of nineteen by the Bishop of Halberstadt. There he taught for almost fifteen years at the canonry just outside the gates of the city. In 1140, although still only in his mid-forties, he had only a year to live. But he had already completed his *opus magnum, On the Sacraments of the Christian Religion*.[3] This work can be called the first *Summa* of the Middle Ages. The term itself appears in Hugh's introduction, not only with its old connotation of a concise summary of many details but already carrying the new[4] and more specialized meaning: *brevis quaedam summa omnium*.[5]

Hugh of Saint-Victor, who has rightly been called a "Johannine phenomenon,"[6] stands wholly within the tradition of Dionysius Areopagita. For him, mystic contemplation was the goal of the spiritual life. At the same time he was convinced that knowledge of reality was the prerequisite for contemplation,[7] and that no kind of science exists which is not destined to be turned into contemplation. Each of the seven liberal arts aims to "restore God's image in us."[8] "Learn everything; later you will see that nothing is superfluous."[9] Out of such all-embracing and expansive attitudes Hugh of Saint-Victor's *Summa* was shaped.

Nevertheless, in spite of all the praise it received,[10] it does not seem to have exerted any too great influence in its own century. Probably it was too much in advance of the times. "The classical textbook for the following centuries was not the greatest and best *Summa*, but a mediocre book of sentences, the *libri quatuor sententiarum* of Peter Lombard."[11] Hugh's book was the first example of the new type, the *Summa*, whereas Peter Lombard's book, although written one or two decades later, belonged to the earlier species of "books of sentences."

We have already said that the vast heritage of tradition had first to be put into accessible and comprehensible form, before it could be drawn upon. This was what the books of sentences were for. In their earliest form they were nothing but collections of properly stated "themes" from the works of the Fathers; the elements of official approval and of binding authority were inherent in the idea of the *sentientia*.[12] One of the first collections of this sort was the *sententiae* of Isidore of Seville, written around 600. It turned out, however, that the mere cataloguing of what there was[13] revealed the fact that the traditional stock included material of great diversity, much of it contradictory. Hence a new task presented itself, one which could not be accomplished by mere assemblage of quotations. Rather, a way had to be found to comprehend these multifarious opinions, which at first glance seemed to be mutually exclusive. Commentators would have to explain these contradictions on grounds of the multiple meanings of words, or the multiple aspects of the subjects in question.

As testimonies to such efforts we have the newer type of books of sentences such as were written around 1100, in the generation of Abélard's teachers.[14] Abélard himself, as was to be expected, composed a very special collection of this sort. Delighting as he did in epigrammatic phrases, he gave it the title "Yea and Nay" (*Sic et non*). And in fact the book counterposed hundreds of texts from the Church Fathers which seemed as contradictory as yes and no. The most important part of Abélard's *Sic et non*, however, is the preface which gave the rules ("rules of concordance") by which these contradictions could be understood, or eliminated.

Thus in the new books of sentences the literal statement was no longer uncritically accepted as it stood.[15] Along with this aspect of the "new criticism" was another important new approach. Henceforth the traditional stock was examined for completeness. Had this or that question been thoroughly explored, or was there still more to be done with it? This meant deciding on what basis wholeness was to be determined, and how to establish divisions of the whole. It meant, moreover, that even while the tradition was being assimilated, a systematic intellectual approach was also beginning to be applied. Later it would take literary shape as the *Summa*. The work of Peter Lombard, the undisputed "Master of Sentences," has its place in this process of transition.

Here we must say a word to correct a possible misunderstanding. This incessant gathering of texts, this constant preoccupation with the views of others, was not very original activity. That must be granted without cavil. But let it not be thought that this mining of the past indicated a lack of direct interest in the subject matter itself. We would be very wrong to think this. The purpose of the endless references to Augustine and others was not, despite appearances, to come to terms with these writers as historical figures. The authors of the books of sentences were too little rather than too much concerned with the historical Augustine and their other authorities. Rather, their whole thought was to arrive at the illumination of the subject matter to be found in the words of the "ancients." Their concern, that is, was first and foremost with the truth about existence and the universe.[16]

To return to the "Master of Sentences," *Peter Lombard* was born around 1100 in the region of Novara—a Lombard like Lanfranc and Anselm of Canterbury. He studied first in Bologna; then, recommended to Bernard of Clairvaux, he went to Rheims and Paris, where he most probably attended Abélard's lectures. At about the age of forty he became *magister* at the cathedral school of Notre Dame, and two decades later (1159-60) Bishop of Paris. As Bishop of Paris, he was very well situated for winning attention for his *Book of Sentences*. But its success was even more due to a "propaganda campaign"[17] launched by an intrepid and extremely active pupil of his, by the name of Peter of Poitiers. This campaign was extraordinarily effective for two reasons: This Peter of Poitiers taught as a professor at the cathedral school of Notre Dame for nearly forty years; and in addition he became the first chancellor of the University of Paris. Nevertheless, such backing alone does not suffice to explain the "almost incomprehensible attractiveness"[18] of the book —which was, as we have already said, entirely mediocre. Some have even held that Peter Lombard's *Sentences* became one of the most successful textbooks in European intellectual history precisely because it "lacked every trace

97

of genius."[19] Another writer has come to the conclusion that its success must have been "almost pure chance."[20] Pope Innocent III read the book, by way of examining its orthodoxy, which had been called into question. His verdict was that it only reported opinions; he could discover no opinions of the author's at all, neither true nor false ones.[21]

One reason for the success of the *Sentences* may well have been its easy comprehensibility, its calm, unhurried flow, intelligent organization, avoidance of needless subtleties, the good choice of texts in which "the average dimensions of contemporary problems"[22] were set forth —in short, the somewhat boring solidity which is after all one of the prime qualities of a good textbook.

Considered from the point of view of content, Peter Lombard's book can rightly be called a systematically organized "Augustine breviary." It contains one thousand texts from the works of Augustine; these make up nearly four fifths of the whole.[23] The principle of organization, formulated by Peter Lombard at the beginning of the book, likewise came from Augustine[24]: on the one hand there are "things" of immediate reality, *res,* and on the other hand references to immediate reality, or "signs," *signa.* In the realm of immediate reality, furthermore, things are divided up between those which man "uses" (*utitur*) and those which he does not use but which he "enjoys" (*fruitur*). God is the reality whose "enjoyment" (*fruitio*) is the goal of human life. To attain that enjoyment we "use" created things.

There is something great and splendid about this scheme, but it is not consistently followed, nor are its intellectual possibilities fully exploited. (For example, only the Sacraments are adduced as "signs.") Thus Peter

Lombard's *Book of Sentences* underwent a strange transformation in the hands of its most important commentator, Thomas Aquinas[25]: using the same objective context, Thomas constructed another, completely persuasive, and no less wonderful principle of organization.[26]

Thomas, incidentally, was only one of some two hundred and fifty commentators[27] who followed in the trail of the "Master of Sentences" during the next few centuries. "Probably," says Grabmann,[28] "after the Holy Scriptures there is no work in Christian literature that has occupied so large a number of exegetes." This is partly due to the fact that Peter Lombard's *libri sententiarum* were firmly entrenched in the curricula of universities well into the sixteenth century, and that every master of theology began his career as a teacher by elucidating them.

Naturally, the "commentaries on the *Sentences*" which thus arose were not restricted to mere exegesis. They soon developed into independent systematic statements by the commentators themselves, and quite often took on the character of a *Summa*. Two examples may serve for many: the principal work of Duns Scotus, the *Opus Oxoniense,* a work of extremely personal cast, nevertheless was outwardly framed as a commentary on Peter Lombard's *Book of Sentences.* And when Thomas Aquinas left his *Summa theologica* uncompleted, his friend Reginald of Piperno was able, after his death, to supply the missing material from Thomas' early commentary on the *Sentences*—and so well does the material work in that we must look very closely indeed to notice the seam.

VII

Augustinian and Platonic in inspiration,[1] founded upon Peter Lombard's "Augustine breviary," the world view of Western Christianity was at last beginning to be rounded out into a compact system. The receptive attitude of the Books of Sentences was being transformed into the independent thinking of the *Summae*. *The* great institution was taking shape which could properly be entrusted with such a universal interpretation of reality— namely, the university. But at the very moment of consolidation, an upheaval was brewing which would shake this newly acquired world view to its foundations. For those works of *Aristotle* hitherto unknown in the West were translated into Latin, and so entered the ken of Occidental thinkers.

These works meant upheaval because they were not simply an addition of "something new" to the existing stock. Rather, the newly translated writings concealed a challenge which was to cast doubt upon all the cherished precepts of the era. And because this challenge bore the name of "Aristotle," it could not possibly be ignored. The logical works of Aristotle, translated and equipped with a commentary by Boethius, had for centuries been accepted as one of the fundaments of all culture.

Yet this basic and well-known work of Aristotle was only the "Old Logic," that is to say, the theory of concept and judgment.[2] To this were added the tracts on the deductive process, on proof, on disputation, and on fallacies, translated into Latin by a Venetian[3] around 1130. These works, taken together, were called the "New Logic."[4] Yet on the basis of these fragments of the complete works, Abélard made bold to say that Aristotle was the "most perspicacious of all philosophers," *perspicacissimus om-nium*.[5] And John of Salisbury wrote: "The sun seemed to have fallen from the sky when Plato departed from this world; all broke out in lamentations, saying that the beacon of the world had been extinguished. But then when his pupil Aristotle mounted to the master's chair, he shone like a star in early morning; he illuminated the globe . . ." and so forth. This was around 1160, when as yet no one in the West knew Aristotle's *Physics*, not to speak of the *Metaphysics*, the book *On the Soul*, the *Nicomachean Ethics*, and the *Politics*.[6] It was therefore bound to happen, once these books were made accessible, that everyone should turn to them with extremely intense eagerness and anticipation.

But at the time of Peter Abélard and John of Salisbury this challenge had not yet been fully presented. It was, however, approaching along several paths, some of which were indeed curious. For example, it was not only from the Greek that the works of Aristotle were translated (chiefly in Sicily, which had always been a natural mart for material and intellectual exchange with the East); most of the medieval Latin translations of Aristotle go back to *Arabic* translations. "When we speak, with a not wholly unjustifiable pride, of the achievements of Western culture," writes Gilson,[7] "we should never forget what the East has contributed to it . . . medieval Europe did not inherit Greek philosophy directly [that is, from Greece], but indirectly, through the channel of Syrian, Persian, and Arabic scholars, scientists, and philosophers." But why, we may ask ourselves, was it not possible to translate the writings of Aristotle directly from the Greek into the Latin, as was done with the works of Dionysius the Areopagite by Irish and Frankish monks as early as the ninth century?

Should anyone answer this question by saying that the very existence of the Dionysius translation stood in the way of a translation of Aristotle, he would not be entirely wrong. During the first millennium, the Christian idea, represented above all by Augustine, was far closer to the Platonic outlook than to the Aristotelian mode of thought. This very state of affairs was in process of radical change around the middle of the twelfth century. The work of someone like John of Salisbury[8] is an example of the change. Here was a wholly new readiness to open the mind to the concrete reality of the world. Western thought was evolving toward the point of view which constitutes the distinctive feature of Aristotelian philosophizing.

In saying this, of course, we have not told the story of why the writings of Aristotle were, fantastically enough, translated from the Arabic; above all, we have not said how Aristotle came into the possession of the Arabs. The answer to this latter question is: by way of political exiles. It is the same answer that explains the route taken by Ionian philosophy from the coast of Asia Minor to Sicily and southern Italy, and finally to Athens; or that today explains why the great centers of symbolic logic are American universities.

The initial alienation between Aristotelian and Christian thought, which had sprung from a multitude of factors, understandably took a sharper turn in the fifth century, when Nestorianism became something of a menace. Nestorianism struck up an open alliance with the philosophy of Aristotle. Nestorius was a Persian by birth. His doctrines bore the impress of the theological school of Antioch. He interpreted the event of God's incarnation in a manner which laid chief stress upon the concrete historical reality, the visible appearance, and hence the human aspect of Christ. It should be clear that the very attempt to do this betrays a certain kinship with the Aristotelian world view. A center of Nestorianism, and characteristically of Aristotelian philosophy also, was the school of Edessa in Syria, the fame of which had spread to far parts of the world during the decades around 400. After the Christological doctrine of Nestorius was condemned as heretical at the Council of Ephesus (431), it could no longer be taught publicly within the boundaries of the Roman Empire. The majority of those affected by the decree of the Council, the "heretics" and also—in so far as they were not identical with these, the "Aristotelians"—left Edessa and emigrated to neighboring Persia. Most of them appear to have remained in Nisibis, just across the border, where soon an equally famous school sprang up, with about a thousand students. (In fact, it was on the model of this school that Cassiodorus, a century later, planned the founding of a university in Rome.[9]) Thus the schools and monasteries of the Nestorian Christians in Syria formed the shelter in which, at that period, the philosophical and scientific writings of the Greeks were preserved and passed on—especially the Aristotelian branch of that heritage. This included not only Aristotle himself, but also Euclid, Hippocrates, Galen, and Archimedes. The philosophical, mathematical, and medical works of those writers appear first to have been translated from Greek into Syrian, then later— possibly by way of intermediary translations into Persian —into the Arabic language. For Islam overwhelmed the entire Near East, including the Persian Sassanid kingdom, and the Aristotelian scholars who were called to the court of the Caliph of Baghdad were mostly Syrians and Persians. By 800 Arabic had become virtually an international language of science. Once translated into Arabic, Aristotle penetrated to the limits of Islam's dominion—which meant, to the Indus in the East and to the Pyrenees in the West.

Within this cultural sphere, then, were written the great commentaries on Aristotle whose authors are mentioned on almost every page of the theological *Summae* of the thirteenth century: *Avicenna,* born in Persia in 980, personal physician to sovereigns, but also philosopher and theologian. According to his own account,[10] he read Aristotle's *Metaphysics* forty times without finding the key to a proper understanding of it. He learned the text by heart—and only then did the meaning of the whole suddenly come to him (an event which he celebrated by a distribution of lavish gifts to the poor). *Averroës,* born in 1126 in Córdoba; jurist, doctor, and philosopher, and to the West in the thirteenth century "the" commentator on Aristotle. His influence in the Latin West was so tremendous that the philosophy of the European Renaissance has with some degree of justice been called "Averroism"—in itself an indication of the direction in which that influence operated.

Strangely enough, these Arabic thinkers influenced Western philosophy and theology far more powerfully than they influenced Islam. In the history of Islam there is no such thing as a "discovery of Aristotle." Rather, Islamic theology is restricted to the Koran, and its history is largely the story of its resistance to philosophy.[11]

A third great name is that of *Moses Maimonides,* likewise born in Córdoba (1135)—a vigorous adherent of the Aristotelian world view, but likewise a firmly orthodox

Jew—and hence confronted by the same unending task which preoccupied the great doctors of medieval Christianity. Most of his books were written in Hebrew, but for his principal work, *Guide for the Perplexed,* he employed Arabic. This book addressed those whose faith in Biblical Revelation had been shaken by philosophy and science. In the opinion of Moses Maimonides, such persons could be led back to their faith only by consistent use of scientific and philosophical arguments. Plainly, then, he too was concerned expressly with the conjunction of faith and knowledge—for which reason Moses Maimonides' book has been called a "Jewish-scholastic *Summa.*"[12]

Here on the one hand was a great wealth of Arabic-Jewish philosophy; and on the other hand the schools of the West were at the same time producing little of value, aside from strictly theological studies. The education available at the Faculty of Liberal Arts in Paris around 1200 rested chiefly on the "cult of logic"[13] and "contained nothing that even remotely resembled a philosophical view of the whole of reality."[14] When we consider this situation, it immediately becomes obvious that Arabic-Jewish philosophy was bound to overwhelm the West with the elemental power of a natural force.

Here is the point at which we must speak in more detail of the translations from the Arabic. At the time that Averroës and Moses Maimonides were born in Córdoba, in southern Spain, the northern half of the Iberian Peninsula had already been liberated from Moorish rule. Toledo, for example, the capital of Visigothic Spain, was reconquered in 1085, and from then until the age of Charles V remained one of the dominant cities of the country. The receding wave of Islam, however, left behind a Spain intellectually changed in many respects, although its basic Christian substance remained inviolate. One sign of these changes was the school of translation which was founded in the twelfth century by a far-sighted Bishop of Toledo. This remarkable school, the only one of its kind in Europe, lasted for several generations, and through its enterprise the great works of Arabic-Jewish Aristotelianism, and above all the works of Aristotle himself, were translated into Latin. But what a tortuous route: translated from the Greek into Syrian, thence (perhaps) into Persian, thence into Arabic!

By chance we happen to know the well-nigh incredible method by which *The Book of the Healing of the Soul*, Avicenna's great work, was "transported" from Arabic to Latin in Toledo around 1140. The translation was the joint work of Dominicus Gondisalvi, who has also left philosophical writings of his own, and of a Jew named Avendehut, who has furnished us with an account of the procedure that was followed. He, knowing Arabic and Castilian (Spanish), translated the individual Arabic words, *singula verba,* into Castilian, whereupon they were again singly translated into Latin by his associate.[15] "It is amazing," we read in Überweg's *History of Philosophy*,[16] "that given this mechanical procedure an intelligible text nevertheless emerged in many cases."

Still, these curious stumbling blocks did not essentially impede the triumphal penetration of the Aristotelian world view into Western thought.[17] With the fashion for Aristotelianism, a number of pseudo-Aristotelian writings were translated into Latin. Of one of these, bearing the highly un-Aristotelian title of *Secret of Secrets*, it has been said[18] that it won Aristotle greater prestige in the "wider public" than did his authentic works. In this work it was stated, for example, that God Himself called Aristotle "an angel rather than a man," and finally took him to Himself in a pillar of light. But of far more consequence was another fact: that Aristotle came to the West accompanied by his Arabic commentators. And that meant that he entered the purview of Western Christianity along with a definite, systematized interpretation.

Given that situation, two outcomes might be expected. Both were only too natural. The first was the tremendous eagerness with which the Aristotelian theory of reality was seized upon and snapped up—for in this branch of philosophy there was nothing remotely approximating it in quality and force. The second was a natural reaction, a concern lest the continuity of tradition and the totality of truth be shattered by the violence of the process of assimilation. Both attitudes were characteristic of the first half of the thirteenth century; and both were frequently intermingled in the strangest fashion.

Thus, on the one hand, between 1210 and 1263 there was a long succession of ecclesiastical admonitions, restrictions, and bans directed against public lectures in universities on Aristotle, particularly against his physics, psychology, and metaphysics.[19] Incidentally, it was not true that "the Church" or an ecclesiastic bureaucracy stood opposed to a solid front of scholars. Rather, there was a powerful group among the university teachers themselves who resisted this disturbing innovation. It would soon become apparent that the ecclesiastical authorities had no intention of identifying themselves with such conservatism on principle.

On the other hand, without revolutionary proclamations or bitter polemics, there developed a constant, consistent, increasingly overt disregard of those prohibitions. Scholars plunged into intensive study of the works of Aristotle, and dealt with these in public lectures at the universities. In a manner that is occasionally difficult to understand, opposition and acceptance often went hand in hand. For example, the bans on Aristotle had not yet been lifted at the time that Thomas Aquinas, who was certainly in complete harmony with the Church, spoke in terms of high praise and with utter matter-of-factness in his first treatise on "the" philosopher, and also of "the" commentator (Averroës). On the other hand, the same Pope Urban IV who in 1263 repeated the earlier warnings and prohibitions had the works of Aristotle translated anew from the Greek at his own court in Orvieto. Just as amazing is the following fact, which in a way may be regarded as concluding the whole episode: When in March, 1255—eight years before the renewed insistence on the ban—the Paris Faculty of Arts incorporated in its new curriculum all the works of Aristotle then known, there was not the slightest protest—"neither on the part of the episcopal authority, nor on the part of theologians, nor on the part of the Pope. The prohibition against lectures on Aristotle had fallen into oblivion. That had been the case perhaps for the past decade; and no one in Paris at the time thought of reviving it." Fernand van Steenberghen, who wrote these sentences,[20] adds, to be sure, the significant remark that the curriculum of 1255 thereby implanted in the receptive soil of the Paris Faculty of Arts that seed from which an anti-Christian, "heterodox" brand of Aristotelianism was very soon to sprout.

VIII

Albertus Magnus was "the first theologian of the Middle Ages who looked Aristotelianism squarely and keenly in the face."[1] With the uncommon hunger for reality which was characteristic of the man, Albert set about on his own[2] to toil through and assimilate the complete works of Aristotle. Bellicose young Roger Bacon would later comment sarcastically on this Paris professor who wanted to teach without himself having been taught. But at that time there existed neither teacher nor a school for the knowledge that Albert wanted to acquire.

Although he himself knew no Greek,[3] he conceived the almost fantastic plan of making the complete works of Aristotle, with their wholly new theory of reality, accessible to the Latin West; *nostra intentio est, omnes dictas partes facere Latinis intelligibiles*.[4] With a similar self-assured statement Boethius, seven hundred years earlier, had announced almost the same intention.[5] Unlike Boethius, however, Albert in his commentaries on all the works of Aristotle actually carried out this resolve. And he did so with a tremendous "irate vigor," fiercely attacking difficulties and often discharging his wrath in a crude and noisy manner against "people who know nothing, but who fight the study of philosophy in every possible way; rude beasts who utter howls against things of which they understand nought."[6] The Swabians of South Germany are celebrated for that kind of invective, and Albert was in fact by birth a Swabian.

The exact year of his birth apparently cannot be determined; probably it fell within the last five years of the twelfth century. During his early studies in Bologna and Padua he fell under the influence of that "catcher of men," Jordan of Saxony, against whom professors were in the habit of warning their students, though with no great success.

Jordan of Saxony, who came from the vicinity of the city of Dassel in Lower Saxony, entered the Dominican Order while St. Dominic was still living, having been won over by the saint himself. Two years afterward, barely thirty years of age, Jordan was elected to succeed the founder as leader of the entire order; a scant fifteen years later he met his end in a storm off the Syrian coast and was buried in Acre. Jordan was one of the most dramatic personalities of the early thirteenth century. His exciting life breathes the turbulence of heroic poetry. His talent for organization and elemental forcefulness in action, combined with extraordinary personal charm,[7] resulted in the founding of hundreds of new monasteries of his order all the way from Ireland to Russia within the few years of his leadership. It was chiefly owing to him that the professors as well as the scholars of the new universities poured into the order founded by St. Dominic. It is said that as soon as he entered a university city, his first act was to order the making of new Dominican habits; and the story goes that he once pawned his own books in order to pay the debts of students entering the order.

It was this man, then, who had himself been a Dominican only for three years, who persuaded Albert to enter the preaching order. Albert, after concluding his theological studies, taught for about ten years in various German monasteries. In 1242 he became the first German to hold a chair at the University of Paris. At that time he signed a university document with the name *Albertus Teutonicus*.[8] During those years, also, he encountered his greatest pupil: Thomas Aquinas, then twenty years old, who had just come from Italy. In 1248, the year the foundation stone of the cathedral at Cologne was laid, both men were in that city; Albert was to set up an academy of the Dominican Order there. A few years later Thomas was called to the Paris monastery of Saint-Jacques, and shortly afterward to the university; during these same years Albert embarked on the restless life which marked his last few decades. As head of the German provinces of the order, he travelled through almost all of Europe from Paris to Hungary, and from Rome to the amber coast of the German Baltic, within the span of three years. Then Pope Alexander IV called him to the episcopal seat of the neglected diocese of Regensburg. "We command you therefore that you obey Our or rather God's wishes . . . and betake yourself to that church, in order to guide it with the prudence that God has conferred upon you." Whereupon the general of the order, Humbert of Romans, strongly urged him to refuse this call, arguing that such "commands" from the Pope were mere matters of form and hardly to be taken seriously as obligatory. "Rather would I see my much-loved son upon the bier than upon the episcopal seat."[9] However, Albert went to Regensburg, though only for two years. There, incidentally, the coarsely shod itinerant monk was called the *Bundschuh* (clog). Then the Pope sent him through Germany to preach a crusade. In 1268 the superiors of the order called him to the University of Paris for the second time; as an outstanding intellectual duellist he was needed there for the strife with the extreme "Averroistic" wing of the Aristotelians. But Albert, who as a bishop occupied a rather special position in the order,[10] declined the invitation; in his stead Thomas Aquinas went. Henceforth Albert established his permanent residence at Cologne. But even at the age of seventy-five he was still travelling about incessantly. In 1273 he was in Nijmegen, in 1274 he attended the General Council at Lyons (Thomas Aquinas died on the way there; Bonaventura died during the council). In 1275 Albert was in Strassburg when the citizenry of Cologne sent for him to settle a protracted dispute between the city, the Archbishop, and the Curia; he had already made one such settlement twenty years before. In 1277, now eighty, he went to Paris to prevent the condemnation of a number of doctrinal principles put forward by his great pupil, Thomas.[11] (He did not succeed.) In 1280 he died at Cologne, and was buried there.

It passes understanding how, in a life so filled with external activities, any man could possibly have succeeded in writing down, or even only dictating, the immense body of literary work which will fill forty quarto volumes in the new critical edition of Albert's *Opera omnia*. Moreover, if we compare Albert with the other writers on philosophy and theology of his era, it turns out that "of all the scholastics he collected and assimilated the most comprehensive material."[12] He is the single one among the teachers of the thirteenth century who wrote commentaries not only on the whole of Aristotle, but also on the complete works of Dionysius the Areopagite.[13] He was also acquainted with the Arabs, above all with the writings of Avicenna, for whom he showed a "great preference."[14] His knowledge of Augustine was, as Grabmann has demonstrated, so extensive that he could not have derived it solely from the collections of quotations then current.

Albert was, like Thomas Aquinas after him, guided by two firm resolutions: on the one hand to surrender no part of the traditional stock, neither Holy Scripture nor

Augustine (and therefore not Plato either); and on the other hand to take full and whole possession of the new truths which were just beginning to be graspable.

To be sure, the tremendous abundance of material heaped up in Albert's works was still incommensurate with his powers of assimilation. Mere accretion was one thing; the talent to create a coherence justified by inherent relationships was another. Even Albert was not equal to the task. With good reason critics have spoken of his "unevenness," "dissonance,"[15] and "restive style."[16] The current of his thought, says Joseph Bernhart,[17] sometimes moved "in eddies against itself." Thus, Albert's works may yield quotations which prove that he was "the creator of Christian Aristotelianism,"[18] contrary quotations, on the basis of which we must say that it would be "false to characterize him as an Aristotelian,"[19] that on the contrary he must be called "rather . . . the vigorous continuator of . . . Neo-Platonism."[20] The task of fitting together all these naturally divergent elements into a unitary and ordered intellectual structure in which the individual elements nevertheless did not lose their character —this task waited for another man. Albert's was a nature given more to conquest than to establishing order. The task of integration was left to his pupil, Thomas Aquinas.

So far we have said nothing at all about a special interest of Albert's, something which lends an individual stamp to his personality. But it was more than that. Here was an interest and a direction which was to emerge more clearly in the thirteenth century, and was to develop, in time, into something radically new, and of incalculable consequence. Without this interest Albert appears as an uncommonly well-informed mind, dominating the tremendous library of traditional thought from basement to roof, but still a scholar concerned chiefly with abstract knowledge, confining himself to association with books. There was, however, another side to him altogether, and this is revealed by his authorship of two books, one on botany[21] and one on zoology.[22] On the basis of this, we must arrive at quite another evaluation of Albert. Here was a man who, still in the Middle Ages, was a passionate devotee of empiricism. Here was a man given to direct observation and experiment.

He used his journeys through the Western world to further this interest, and was forever asking questions of fishermen, hunters, beekeepers, and bird-catchers. He himself also bent his sight upon the things of the visible world; he observed with all his senses alert, with extreme precision and lack of "pretensions," in Goethe's sense of the word.[23] He describes an apple[24] from peel to core. He describes with the greatest precision the "evergreen leathery leaves" of the mistletoe, "almost like olive leaves, but with a lemon-yellow gleam."[25] He tells which spiders[26] spin webs and where—by windows, in shrubs, on the ground—and which spiders catch their prey by leaping upon it. He distinguishes between thorns and spikes. He knows, because he had discovered this by tasting, that the sap of trees[27] is bitterest in the roots, and that the bee's abdomen contains a transparent little sac with a subtle taste of honey.[28] He points out that the eel does not live on mud, as Aristotle maintains: "I myself have seen it eat a frog, worms, and pieces of fish, and it can be caught on the hook with such bait."[29] Quite often he corrects[30] Aristotle in this way, that is, by referring back to experience; in particular, of course, he corrects the purely legendary allegations of the chapbook *Physiologus*. He makes such corrections in the tone of one setting up principles; frequently he states his rebukes rather aggressively. For example: "There can be no philosophy about concrete things" —*de particularibus enim philosophia esse non poterit*.[31] Or: "The phoenix is a bird of Eastern Arabia—so we learn from the writings of those who do their researches more in mystical theology than in nature."[32] Here was a mind, then, that prized truth and accuracy. Yet what a gulf between his attitude and that of Philistine "scientificality." We see this in Albert's description of the basic forms of the blossom; here his precise observation is linked with pure poetry. The blossom, says Albert in this book of plants,[33] has three types of form: bird, bell, and star.

When I say that Albert set something new in motion, something of incalculable consequences, I do not mean only because of his remarkable store of empirically acquired knowledge of nature. It is true that even as a scientist his contribution was outstanding, and he made a new beginning: "If the development of the natural sciences had continued on the path set by Albert, a detour of three centuries would have been saved."[34] But the key point of Albert's contribution was this, and it was this which represented an unprecedented advance in a *philosophical* interpretation of the universe: that he declared with unyielding firmness that all natural cognition has to start with the concrete knowledge of reality obtained from direct encounters with the things of the world. Tradition too, in so far as it lays claim to validity, and wherever it concerns matters susceptible to empirical examination, must be able to withstand investigation. That meant nothing less than: as far as experience applies, mature man's independence as against every imaginable authority is self-evident. *Experimentum solum certificat in talibus*[35] —this is a completely new statement, a new claim: "In such matters only experience provides certainty." And it becomes plain that this declaration was framed to oppose and to exclude another approach. We are being told, in other words, that the chief thing is neither the formalisms of logic nor the feats of rational speculation in combining ideas into "syntheses"; what matters is solely *knowledge of the subject* obtained out of experienceable reality. That point of view is quite clearly aimed against those "who consider every distinction of ideas to be an objective solution"—*qui omnem distinctionem solutionem esse reputant.*[36] "As far as I am concerned, I abhor logical arguments in those sciences which have to do with things."[37]

Werner Heisenberg[38] said some time ago that during the Middle Ages "nature was thought of as the work of God," and that "it would have seemed meaningless to the people of those times to inquire into the material world independent of God." In connection with men like Albertus Magnus and Thomas Aquinas that is, to put it mildly, an untenable simplification. Naturally both men were convinced that the world was Creation (*creatura*). But *because* the act of creating things signifies *per definitionem* that the things are truly given their own being, possess being as their property, both Albert and Thomas knew that the works of God cannot be grasped unless they are viewed as what they are in themselves, *secundum quod hujusmodi sunt.*[39] Nobody, before Albertus Magnus, had ever expressed this with such vigorous precision. This was the novelty. Albert simply takes it for granted that theological arguments should be kept out of scientific investigations.[40] Moreover, he had, as Gilson[41] puts it, "no patience with the saintly simplicity of some theologians," who discharge themselves of the obligation to give a philosophical answer to philosophical questions. Rather, he insisted that theologians master and be in command of the philosophical and scientific learning of the time.[42] We can very well understand the dismay of his own order in the face of such almost unfulfillable demands. It was only to be expected that several chapters general (1271, 1278, 1280) should have responded to this disquieting new doctrine by laying stress upon the precedence of theology over profane knowledge.[43] This was only natural for a community of priests. Nevertheless, there can be no question but that Albert for the first time properly posed the true task of theology in the world —even though it may not be possible for this task, any more than philosophy's—to be accomplished in full by any single individual.

Once again, then, a dimension of difficulty has entered into the conjunction of *fides* and *ratio*. The problem has become even more taxing—especially since *ratio* itself has acquired a new and more comprehensive meaning. To Albertus Magnus *ratio* implies not only the capacity for formally correct thinking. Neither is it the power to bring the truths of salvation within reach of our intellects by means of creatural analogies and "reasons of convenience." It implies first and foremost the capacity of man to grasp the reality he encounters. What John of Salisbury practiced, but made no great effort to justify in theory, was formulated as a principle by Albertus Magnus. He based his thinking on the broadest experience with reality, and simultaneously upon a profound knowledge of the whole of contemporary philosophy and theology. "As far as you are able, join faith with reason"—henceforth this sentence of Boethius' would mean the task of bringing belief into a meaningful co-ordination—which must ever and again be shaped anew—with the incessantly and immeasurably multiplying total stock of natural knowledge of man and the universe.

IX

Truth is the self-manifestation and state of evidence of real things. Consequently, truth is something secondary, following from something else. Truth does not exist for itself alone. Primary and precedent to it are existing things, the real. Knowledge of truth, therefore, aims ultimately not at "truth" but, strictly speaking, at gaining sight of reality. Furthermore, when we distinguish "truth of faith" from "truth of reason," we are saying that on the one hand there exist things which we can see only by faith and divine revelation, and on the other hand things which can be apprehended by natural cognition. Even when we speak of "faith" and "knowledge," despite the literal meaning of these words we are not speaking of two different acts or approaches of the human mind, but of two realms of reality which we touch upon when we believe or know.

"Conjunction of faith and knowledge"—at bottom that comes down to mentally uniting these two *realms of reality*: on the one hand the totality of created things which lie within the purview of natural cognition (which does not mean that we ever fully understand them); and on the other hand the reality exposed to us in God's revelations, that is to say, in faith. For this latter reality, we have the code-words "Trinity" and "Incarnation." To interpret the conjunction in this way, however, is also to make a demand that is not directed at the rational intellect alone: to this extent the expression "mentally uniting" is not quite accurate. For what we are called upon to do is not entirely mental; it lies closer to the core of personality than that, and challenges spiritual existence.

This, then, is more or less the interpretation that Thomas Aquinas gave to Boethius' celebrated dictum. It was the most radical formulation which could be given to the idea. With that consistency absolutely distinctive in him, Thomas sees natural reality as divine creation which in the event of the Incarnation has been reunited, in an incomprehensibly new way, with its Origin.

And in seeing and saying this, he makes two things plain: first, that man's turning toward all aspects of the world is an attitude not only justified but required by theology—very much so; and second, that theology itself can develop only within the framework of total reality, and that not one single element of that total reality can be excluded from consideration. As we summed it up once before[1]: "theologically based worldliness, and a theology open to the world."

From the start we may well surmise that this conception is not easily carried out in practice. It will therefore not be the rule. Where it is so carried out, by a fortunate providence, we can scarcely expect that so improbable a condition, in which opposing forces are held in equilibrium, will be of long duration. Gilson[2] has spoken of the "moment" which must be assigned to the "classical period" in the development of scholasticism—a moment immediately before the impending storm whose coming could well be sensed by everyone. It was almost possible to deduce in advance and *in abstracto* the probable directions in which the highly differentiated and consequently highly vulnerable ordered structure was likely to "give" and break up.

For example, it could be predicted that someone would come along (or rather, that someone was lying in wait all the time) to say: "I by no means disapprove of the study of philosophy (and the sciences), so long as it serves the theological mystery. . . ." These words, expressly aimed at Thomas Aquinas' commentaries on Aristotle, were written by his adversary, the Franciscan *John Peckham*,[3] professor at the Universities of Paris and Oxford, later Archbishop of Canterbury. John Peckham belongs among the spokesmen of the traditional philosophic-theological view which has customarily been called (though the designation is not a very happy one) "medieval Augustinism."[4] His objection amounts to this: that the theologian needs to know only a part of creation; there are, after all, important and unimportant things in the world, and to achieve the conjunction of *fides* and *ratio* only what is pertinent to the subject really counts. This thesis was a thoroughly natural one for a professor of theology to hold. It elicited the support of the general of the Franciscan Order, Bonaventura, who came forth strongly in its defense during the last years of his life. His dominant concern was for the unity of the Christian view of the universe, and experience with extreme Aristotelianism at the University of Paris had made him more mistrustful of the qualities of natural reason than he had been earlier.[5]

Thomas, also a theologian, answered this objection in

somewhat this way: No one is competent to determine what natural things are important or unimportant for theology to know; the "benefit" the theologian may derive from investigation of the real world cannot be measured in advance; but in general it can be said that faith pre-supposes and therefore needs natural knowledge of the world.[6] At times, no doubt, an error concerning the created world leads men astray from the truth of faith also.[7] Finally, moreover, the study of created things must be praised for its own sake,[8] since these things are works of God.

Incidentally, John Peckham links his objection with still other arguments which are more relevant to it than may appear. For example, the famous public debate waged by Thomas Aquinas and John Peckham in 1270, before the professors and students of Paris, centered around the thesis, advocated by Thomas and passionately rejected by his opponent,[9] that only a single principle of life exists in man—namely, the spiritual soul. To put this question in a somewhat less scholastic way, Thomas was maintaining and Peckham denying that the body is part and parcel of the nature of man.[10] At this point it becomes very clear what part of Creation it was which this un-worldly theology considered to be "less important," if not quite suspect.

But Peckham, that representative of the conservatives' fundamental unworldliness, was not the most dangerous of the opponents whom Thomas found himself confronting. More destructive, more fraught with consequences, and perhaps more obvious and inevitable, was the threat to his conception from rabid secularists: an avant-guard-istic group of young Parisian professors who from about

1265 on congregated around their impulsive colleague *Siger of Brabant.*

Various catchwords have been proposed for this group: "Latin Averroism,"[11] "heterodox Aristotelianism,"[12] "philosophism."[13] We will not comment upon these designations, each of which appears to underline one aspect of the matter. But what were the theses advocated by this group? A whole list of them could be set down (eternity of the world; singularity of the intellect in all men; denial of freedom of the will; etc.). The common factor in them, however, is difficult to grasp; it seems to be concealed under a kind of camouflage. Their questioning of tradition was plainly so radical that they did not dare to state it bluntly—perhaps not even to themselves.[14] One of the most useful ruses was to fall back on the interpretation of Aristotle. "Among those who labor in philosophy, some say things which are not true according to faith; and when told that what they say goes against faith, they reply that it is the Philosopher [Aristotle] who says so; as for themselves, they do not affirm it, they are only repeating the Philosopher's words." Thus Thomas Aquinas in a sermon at the University of Paris.[15] As we see, this is not so remote from a charge of "double truth," from accusing Siger of Brabant and his fellows of holding the opinion that a thing could be true scientifically and philosophically, and at the same time theologically false —and vice versa. Now it is quite certain that Siger of Brabant not only did not advocate the doctrine of double truth, but expressly rejected it. And there is much evidence that he did so in all sincerity, not out of mere caution.[16] But in this regard I would hold with Gilson[17] that it comes to the same thing; many a man, subjectively, with utter sincerity, has rejected a conclusion which he nevertheless affirms "in principle." Considered in purely logical terms, at any rate, there was scarcely any way for Siger of Brabant to escape the conclusion of double truth. Which meant that here for the first time since Boethius, indeed since Augustine and Justin, the way was open to deny the principle of conjoining what was believed with what was known—to repudiate *the principle itself*. In that repudiation the end of the Middle Ages was foreshadowed.

Nevertheless, we cannot say that Siger of Brabant was concerned with a formal repudiation of the principle. In general, he was not primarily interested in negations—that is obvious. When we consider everything that the research of recent decades has brought to light concerning the work of this man,[18] we can see behind his various doctrines and theses a single passionate interest. Perhaps the word should be not "interest" but "fascination." It was a fascination—quite understandable in a man so enthusiastically dedicated to the process of thinking—with the truly amazing potentialities of human reason to acquire knowledge and insight. Those potentialities had suddenly been revealed to Siger and his contemporaries by Aristotle, and seemed in the first rush of enthusiasm utterly without limit. Aristotle had newly brought within the range of their vision the wealth of the natural world, the infinite possibilities of exploring it. "Even more than reason, it seems to have been nature that Aristotle opened up to these minds"; "there came to light a *real* world, a *knowable* world."[19]

And what about theology? Of course it was not expressly denied; such denial was simply beyond the bounds of possibility for the thought of that age. But in the face of this new plethora of knowledge about the natural world, theology simply became uninteresting. With a kind of naïve nonchalance and ruthlessness, it was left to itself.[20] The fact is that Siger of Brabant, who was, after all, Canon of St. Martin's in Liége, wrote not a single tractate on a theological theme, although he was the author of a considerable body of work.[21] That, too, was something new, something *"un*-medieval."

From about 1265 on, then, a dynamic rationalism began to dominate the field at the University of Paris. Reason began to plume itself on its autarchy. And at the time there was no one in the city of Paris who could oppose such rationalism with superior arguments. Hence it was that Albertus Magnus was called to Paris, and when he refused, Thomas Aquinas was again sent for (1268). And Thomas vigorously intervened in the dispute. He had, however, to wage on several fronts, without any real allies,[22] a battle as theoretically difficult as it was practically dangerous. For he had to fight the revolutionaries around Siger of Brabant, and simultaneously the convinced conservatives of the type of John Peckham—from whose point of view Siger and Thomas were actually one and the same, each equally dangerous and for the same reason. "In the sight of those who could not understand the deeper meaning of his philosophical innovations, Thomas Aquinas was bound to appear, if not as an Averroist, at least as a fellow traveller."[23] Thomas also argued, in his lesser polemic writings,[24] against particular doctrines of Siger of Brabant. But above all during those years in Paris, which were to be the last years of his life, he wrote the great commentaries on Aristotle. They show to what extent he himself, no less than Siger of Brabant and his fellows, likewise considered the natural world to be a "good" reality in its own right, deserving affirmation of all its aspects. And he thought this not in spite of theological reasons but for the very best theological reasons: because he understood the world as Creation and, moreover, as the *materia* of Christianity's sacramental mysteries. It seems, however, that Thomas did not succeed in making clear to his adversaries that this conception preserved the best in the mutually opposing doctrines. Above all, he apparently failed to convince them that his own position differed radically from that of Siger of Brabant, quite aside from differences in particular points of doctrine. The advocates of the traditional Augustinian-Platonic world view, at any rate, would continue to deny that there was any such difference. And with Siger himself the difficulty was that his deepest convictions remained unexpressed for various reasons (caution? self-delusion? camouflage?), and therefore scarcely to be grasped. If he were "pinned down," he would answer that what he was putting forth was not his own doctrines, but interpretation of Aristotle. Nor could anyone charge that reason was being allowed to claim far too exclusive validity. For Siger and his fellows would hasten forward with the assurance that if any disharmony between faith and knowledge appeared, of course faith deserved the precedence.[25]

A word remains to be said about one peculiarity of this new rationalism which at first sight appears strange and positively irrational. F. van Steenberghen[26] speaks of the "curious fact" [*chose curieuse*] that "these bold and revolutionary spirits who did not hesitate to shatter the ideas they had received from their Christian environment should simultaneously have subscribed to a veritable cult of philosophical tradition," so that philosophizing meant to them above all "to investigate what the philosophers thought about any particular question."[27] As may easily be seen, this is something which we might call highly contemporary, for this sort of purely historical examination of philosophical questions is much the fashion nowadays. However, to my mind there is nothing curious about it; it is what one would naturally expect to happen. For the very moment anyone engaged in philosophizing abandons the guidance of sacred tradition, two things happen to him. The first is that he loses sight of his true subject, the real world and its structure of meaning, and finds himself instead talking about something entirely different: philosophy and philosophers. The second is that he forfeits his legitimate hold on the solely binding tradition, and must therefore illegitimately and—it must be said—vainly seek support in the mere facts handed down to him, in whatever historical "material" happens to be at his disposal, following the "great thinkers" whom he has encountered more or less by chance, or occupying himself industriously with the opinions of other people.

Here we must recall to mind the dictum of St. Thomas,[28] concerning this very matter, addressed in 1271-72 to Siger of Brabant, and since cited many times: "The purpose of the study of philosophy is not to learn what others have thought, but to learn how the truth of things stands."

X

The discussions of medieval philosophy published after 1950 are distinguished from almost all earlier works of this type by (among other things) their attributing a surprisingly high degree of importance to a particular

126

event which at first sight seems to have been not especially noteworthy: the ecclesiastical condemnation pronounced in March, 1277, in Paris and Oxford against certain philosophical and theological propositions. In Albert Stöckl's three-volume *Geschichte der Philosophie des Mittelalters* (1864-66) the fact is mentioned only casually. The otherwise detailed account in Überweg's history[1] (1928 edition) spends a bare twenty lines upon the matter. On the other hand, Fernand van Steenberghen's history[2] of doctrinal development in the thirteenth century devotes an entire chapter to it, almost a fifth of the entire text. And of the eleven parts into which Étienne Gilson divides his 1955 *History of Christian Philosophy in the Middle Ages,* one is headed: "The Condemnation of 1277."

Van Steenberghen calls this "most important condemnation of the Middle Ages"[3] the "true pivot of the intellectual history of this epoch."[4] Gilson speaks of a "landmark," and says that the event changed the atmosphere of intellectual life so fundamentally that without further ado we can tell whether certain doctrines were conceived before it or after it.[5]

What was it that happened?

When Thomas Aquinas left Paris in 1272 and died a year and a half later, the conflict of opinions on the role of philosophy and the "secular" sciences continued—as was to be expected. One thing, however, had changed: the position taken by St. Thomas no longer had a defender of his rank—although strictly speaking he had never been "partisan" in this conflict.

In 1276 Petrus Hispanus—born in Lisbon, at one time professor of logic in Paris, commentator on Aristotle and Dionysius the Areopagite, and incidentally also a physician of the Greco-Arabic school—ascended to the papal throne as John XXI. Naturally interested in the doctrinal disputes at Paris, he asked the Bishop of Paris, Étienne Tempier, for a report. But this Bishop, who only a few years before had himself been a professor at the University of Paris, was, to put it mildly, thoroughly "committed"; he belonged to the traditional party, which is to say that he flatly rejected Siger of Brabant, but also had considerable reservations toward Thomas Aquinas. Whether he ever sent the requested report to Rome can no longer be determined; there are no traces of any such document. At any rate, Bishop Tempier was an impetuous man and "not exactly the soul of moderation."[6] He hurriedly assembled a commission and had a "hasty investigation"[7] carried out. Only six weeks after the date of the papal inquiry—and thus before a reply from Rome to any report that may have been sent could have reached him— the Bishop published a list of two hundred and nineteen propositions which by virtue of his own authority he condemned. This list was published on March 7, 1277— exactly three years to the day after the death of Thomas Aquinas. That fact is worth mentioning because the condemnation decretal included a number of doctrines of the man who was later to be regarded as the "universal teacher" of the Church. (Since there were no literal citations from Thomas' writings, precise identification was difficult, and as a matter of fact is still a contested question. Gilson[8] comments ironically on the situation: "The list of the Thomistic propositions involved in the condemnation is longer or shorter according as it is compiled by a Franciscan or by a Dominican.")

The condemnation lumped together propositions of the most various content "in handsome disorder," as van

Steenberghen[9] says, and by no means avoiding repetitions and even contradictions. The propositions deal with the meaning of philosophy, with divine cognition, with the relationship between Creator and Creation, with the angels, with miracles, with the ultimate goal of man, and so on. Nevertheless, the gist of this condemnation was made fairly plain, if only by the fact that the Bishop in his preface spoke bluntly of professors of the Faculty of Arts who followed pagan philosophers and advocated abominable errors, but who then, in order to avoid the charge of heresy, presumed a difference between the truth of faith and philosophical truth "as if there could be two mutually contradictionary truths"—*quasi sint duae contrariae veritates.*[10]

Naturally, Bishop Tempier's jurisdiction did not extend beyond the diocese of Paris. Nevertheless, the University of Paris was subject to his authority, and that is what matters here. Now, however, a further step was taken: just eleven days after the Paris condemnation the Archbishop of Canterbury for his part condemned a series of propositions. And naturally Canterbury itself was not what mattered, but the university which lay within the diocese of Canterbury: Oxford University. Moreover, all the propositions condemned in Oxford could be regarded as more or less "Thomistic."[11] In this connection it is necessary for us to know that the Archbishop of Canterbury, Robert Kilwardby—likewise former *magister* at Paris, and subsequently professor of theology in Oxford —was, although a Dominican, nevertheless a determined opponent of Thomas Aquinas, fellow member of his order. Kilwardby's successor to the archiepiscopal seat at Canterbury was to be none other than John Peckham, who in 1284 once again expressly confirmed the condemnation and in 1286 followed it up with a second, also directed against Thomas.

Such, then, are the facts, put in summary form. These events took on particular importance because their scene was set at the two leading academies of Christendom. Evidently this setting was not a matter of chance, but corresponded precisely to the intentions of the two bishops, who could scarcely have been acting without a concerted plan. And, indeed, the condemnations stirred up extraordinary excitement throughout the West. In Paris, the Oxford decree was discussed just as animatedly as Bishop Tempier's order. And within a very short time Robert Kilwardby had to give his opinion on a critical inquiry addressed to him by another Dominican, also a Bishop (of Corinth). This was Peter of Conflans. Kilwardby replied by referring to the support of the Oxford professors—having previously assured himself that he had it.[12]

From these facts alone it is evident that the most varied forces and motives, scarcely to be disentangled, were at play—for which reason an accurate estimate of the events is by no means easy. Certainly, anyone who insists upon seeing the whole affair merely as a clerical or professorial intrigue is losing sight of the chance to obtain a wider and more comprehensive understanding of the situation. Rivalries undeniably played a considerable part; when we read, in an extremely learned treatise on Bishop Tempier, that the decree of 1277 was, in so far as it concerned Thomas Aquinas, a tendentious partisan plot,[13] we may be sure that this is no facile judgment. Moreover, it can scarcely be denied that the Paris condemnation was a measure of defense on the part of the Theological Faculty against the increasing fame and influence of the Faculty of Arts. Van Steenberghen[14] has called the condemnation an "ill-considered action, provoked by the panic among the theologians, and perhaps also by the growing success of Aristotelianism."

Yet we must not overlook the fact that the condemnation was simultaneously a disciplinary act on the part of ecclesiastical authority, directed against what amounted to secularism in principle which, *nota bene,* was being taught by professors who were clerics or priests at a university founded upon papal privileges. It seems to me that the Church cannot very well be gainsaid the right to act in this way. And in saying this we turn our attention from personal motivations or inadequacies, and to the objective justification for the decree.

Let us put aside for a moment the circumstances in which the condemnation came into being. Instead, let us fasten our attention on the condemned propositions. What was it that they stated? Viewed with a minimum of bias, this is what they came down to: that felicity is to be sought in this, not in another, life; that the Christian religion hinders learning; that the soul of man is inseparably bound to the body; that creation out of nothing is impossible; that the practice of theology in no way enlarges one's knowledge; that there is no state finer than devotion to philosophy. If we can duly, without prejudice, take note of all this, then we scarcely know what else the official Church might have done, except to declare authoritatively: These propositions are in opposition to Christian doctrine.

There is need here, it seems to me, for a brief note on the meaning and the legal status of ecclesiastical "condemnations" in general—since the modern mind is prone to rebel outright if it is asked to do anything so outrageous as to take such "hopelessly medieval" things in other than a historical way. Granted, the subject is somewhat complicated—at any rate not so simple as the modern intellectual with his stereotyped reaction supposes. I shall confine myself to offering a few points for consideration.

First: If there is something like "Revelation," that is to say, speech of God audible to man, in which something is made known which is not knowable in any other way (I am not speaking of *whether* there is Revelation; yet it is clear that Christianity rests upon this fundamental assumption; but even in the pre- and extra-Christian worlds, in Plato, for example, there has always been a living conviction that "divine speech," *theios logos,* exists); and if—*secondly*—what is revealed in the divine speech is not immediately accessible to every man, if rather this Everyman must depend upon the divine speech's being communicated and passed on, "handed down as tradition" from generation to generation by those who first received it (those who partook of "inspiration," the "Prophets," and the "Ancients")—if these things are so, then it is simply in the nature of the thing that not everyone is capable of interpreting the meaning of the Revelation. Not everyone can know what was truly meant by it. It is necessary to conceive a definitive authority of some kind which not only preserves and passes on the tradition, but also gives a binding interpretation to it; an authority which, for example, also says what was *not* meant by the divine speech, and what is incompatible with it. Precisely that is the meaning of such "condemnations." Like theology as a whole, they are a matter fundamentally fraught with conflict (indeed, that is to be expected), for one reason because the interpretation of the Revelation (which can be binding in many different degrees) is itself subject to the conditions of history. Nevertheless, if and as long as men retain the conviction that God has revealed Himself to those He has chosen, they will consider it imperative that this Revelation be protected against all pollution and all misinterpretation.

Now as for the so easily dismissed "medievalism" of this point of view: the Middle Ages would in fact never have accepted a formal dogmatization or even a condemnation of doctrines which rested upon purely human authority, without any connection with divine Revelation. As everyone will realize, we are here touching upon a phenomenon that has become a daily occurrence in the totalitarian world these days, where "deviations" are constantly being condemned with an absolute claim to rightness—but *without* appeal to a standard of truth which alone can properly uphold authoritarian claims. No such appeal is possible, nor is it even thought necessary.[15] Men like Thomas Aquinas, or even Bishop Tempier, or Robert Kilwardby, would regard such authoritarian claims as not only a violation of the dignity of human reason, but also and above all as an absurdity from the theoretical point of view. On the other hand, the sorry fact remains that in these times of ours there are not a few secularized intellectuals who accept both the degradation of dignity and the absurdity. . . . All this as an aside from the subject of "condemnation of propositions."

Quite another matter from the question of authorization is the question of whether that disciplinary act, the condemnation of 1277, alleviated and settled the long-smoldering unrest into which the thinking of Western Christendom had been thrown by the encounter with the superior Greco-Arabic knowledge of the world and the interpretation of reality based upon it. Our immediate reaction may be that the condemnation rather stood in the way of a genuine clarification and arbitration. What Thomas and Albert had in fact said, in the face of the assault of Greco-Arabic wisdom, was this: Let us accept what is *true* in it, as an enrichment, and add to it (and co-ordinate with it!) what truth we, as knowers and as believers, already possess; but we will refute what is false in it.

All very well. But what would happen when there was no one capable of or willing to carry out that refutation and co-ordination? It is, consequently, not easy to say what would have happened if the radical decision of 1277 had not taken place in Paris and Oxford.

In terms of the academic dispute, at any rate, and the dynamics of scholarly life, the effects of the decree appear to have been extremely upsetting. For half a century—so van Steenberghen comments[16]—the life of the University of Paris was paralyzed by this set of proscriptions; even within the boundaries of orthodoxy, the free play of ideas was checked.[17] Naturally, the dispute between "Aristotelianism" and "Augustinism" went on. But it began to degenerate from a fruitful controversy to a sterile wrangle, with the debaters more concerned with being right than in finding the truth. A controversy is really possible only between individual minds; and the rules of the game call for each of the debaters to concede points to the others, that is to say, to accept the stronger argument, even if it comes from an adversary. Such reasonable exchanges became steadily more improbable because the front lines began to solidify; they froze into the organized blocks of "schools" which of late had become pretty much identical with particular religious communities and imposed conformity on all their members. Robert Kilwardby, for example, could still come forth as an individual to oppose the "Aristotelianism" of Thomas Aquinas, a fellow member of his order. But a year after the Paris and Oxford condemnations, when the general chapter of the Dominicans (at Milan in 1278) had declared the teachings of Thomas Aquinas to be the official doctrine of the order, conduct like Kilwardby's would have been a breach of discipline.

This, then, was the great change. The event of 1277 did not produce it, but allowed it to take shape all at once, like the precipitation of crystals which have long been forming. In Gilson's[18] opinion, the change was of such far-reaching significance that it must actually be considered to mark the end of an epoch. Above all, Gilson argues, the Christian world view, which of course has always been simultaneously theological and philosophical, went over to the defensive as against "worldly" knowledge; anxious suspicion took the place of the former friendly co-operation.

On the distant horizon could be discerned the opposition between on the one hand a theology which distrusted *ratio,* and on the other hand that attitude of mind which Dilthey[19] has characterized as the "atheism of scientific thinking."

The "golden age of scholasticism," the "honeymoon of theology and philosophy had then come to an end."[20]

An even farther-reaching significance must, it appears, be ascribed to the condemnation of 1277. But that meaning becomes evident only when we trace backward the connection of that decree with Boethius, Anselm, and Abélard, and forward with *Duns Scotus,* of whom we are about to speak. Geological formations on the surface of the earth can be distinguished from a great height, though they remain hidden to the nearby view. Just so, when we take a historical perspective and regard the eight-hundred-year span between the birth of Boethius and the death of Thomas Aquinas, we are able to discern a multimembered intellectual configuration in which the event of March, 1277, forms a kind of joint.

The outlines of this configuration can most easily be drawn if we start with Anselm's idea of the *rationes necessariae*—that most trenchant expression of a conception also present in the thinking of Boethius and Abélard. Anselm's idea[1] was that the reasoning human mind can use "compelling reasons" to make understandable the events of Salvation, which are known to us through faith. This, however, expressly does *not* mean that we accept the truths of faith only because their necessity appeals to our reason; rather, that faith provides the basis by which we can reach understanding of what we believe. The meaning of Anselm's formula, *credo ut intelligam,* has been shown to be this. Now, however, we must take a somewhat closer look at the logical structure of this "compelling reasoning."

A sentence from *Cur Deus homo,* the work of Anselm's later years, reads thus: "It is therefore necessary that they [the fallen angels] be replaced from human nature, since there is no other [nature] from which they could be replaced."[2] In this sentence the following truths of faith are assumed: There are beings of pure spirit, some of whom decided against God; God has called man to a communion with Himself which exceeds what is man's due from nature. This, then, is the *credo* that underlies the sentence. The rational element in it, the *intelligo,* may be reduced approximately to the following essential elements: There is a rational and perfect number [*rationabilis et perfectus numerus*[3]] of beings called to the contemplation of God; "those angels who fell were created so that they should be contained in this number"[4]; the number can be "filled out" only by spiritual beings; aside from the angels, the only spiritual beings are men; therefore: "since there is no other nature . . ." and so on.

I have already said that the Christian of today is inclined to greet such arguments with very mixed feelings, with a compound of astonishment and extreme discomfiture. Nevertheless, we refer to such arguments, and deliberately evoke that embarrassment, in order to convey more directly the significance of Duns Scotus' position. For we are interested, not in the content, but, as we have said, in the logical validity of the formal chain of ideas, a chain which recurs many times in Anselm's works. Let us then ask: Under what assumption (aside from the revelation of truth assumed by faith) can Anselm's line of argument lay claim to validity? The answer must be: Under the dual assumption that—first—everything which God does must be rational; and that—secondly—man, or more precisely, the believing man, for his part can recognize and prove this rationality.

This idea of Anselm's, however, leads us almost immediately to a further idea: that God is acting under necessity and cannot help acting in a certain way—namely, to do in every case what is most rational; and hence, that in each case the rationality of what He does can be intelligible to the reason of (believing) man; and that, therefore, from the extreme rationality of any idea a conclusion can be drawn as to its actual validity, or rather as to its reality; that, accordingly, to put the matter briefly: everything that is *must* be as it is. Once again: I am not saying that this was Anselm's opinion, but that if Anselm's principle of *rationes necessariae* is taken at its word, it is only a single step to this idea.

This very idea, however, is the common fundamental underlying a great many of the propositions cited for condemnation in the decree of March, 1277, even though it does not come to the surface quite so plainly as in the theses ascribed to Siger of Brabant,[5] which state: that God by necessity brings forth everything that proceeds directly from Him (20); that the Prime Cause can directly cause only a single effect (33); that God cannot create anything additionally new, nor create anything in a new way (22)—which last is linked with the proposition: that in this mortal life we are capable of knowing God in His essence (9). Gilson[6] has spoken of the "Greek necessitarianism" that Avicenna and Averroës inherited from Aristotle; but the connection between the "Averroistic" theses advocated at the University of Paris and the "Aristotelian identification of reality, intelligibility, and necessity, not only in things, but first and above all in God"—the connection of all these individual errors with this fundamental idea of Aristotle was brought to light with perfect distinctness by the condemnation of 1277.[7]

Such "necessitarianism," in so far as it can at all be

meaningfully co-ordinated with the Christian world view, plainly needs a double corrective. One corrective had already been present and effective in Western Christianity for several hundred years, although Anselm himself and the extreme Aristotelians around Siger of Brabant were hardly affected by it: this was the idea of "negative" theology as formulated in the works of Dionysius the Areopagite. The other corrective is contained within a single watchword: *freedom*. This one word was also the battle-cry of Duns Scotus.

"Scotland bore me, England received me, France taught me, Cologne holds me fast." This inscription on the grave of John Duns Scotus in the Minorite Church in Cologne memorializes the stations of his brief life, which ran its course between 1266 and 1308. At the age of fifteen he entered the Franciscan Order; a decade later he was consecrated priest in Northampton; at twenty-seven, after a brief stay in Oxford, he went to Paris for several years of study. Then followed a number of years of teaching, probably in Oxford. A second stay at the University of Paris was interrupted for a short time by a conflict with the King of France. In 1307 he was sent from Paris to Cologne, where he died not long afterward at the age of forty-two. The voluminous works on philosophy and theology that he left, including above all the commentary on the sentences usually cited as the "Oxford Work" (*Opus Oxoniense*), do not seem to have come down to us in wholly authentic texts, although the substance of his thought is there. Because of these textual problems, several scholars[8] maintain that a definitive portrayal of the real Duns Scotus is not yet possible. This may also explain the somewhat divergent interpretations[9] which have been accorded to his doctrine and his personality.

The watchword "freedom," which I said characterized Duns Scotus, refers above all to the freedom of *God*. This may seem to us a purely theological thesis, but we will think otherwise as soon as we see the conclusion which Duns Scotus quickly draws from this: Because God is absolutely free, everything that He does and effects has the character of nonnecessity, of being in a particular sense "accidental" (contingent). This applies both to God's creative work, and therefore to Creation itself, and to the events included within the history of Salvation.

The direction in which this argument aims is quite plain. In a word: there are no "necessary reasons" for the work of God. And certainly human reason is incapable of arriving by deductions and arguments at that which has emerged as the result of a free divine act; human reason cannot claim that such results are meaningful "in themselves," let alone necessarily intelligible. As far as the absolute freedom of God reaches, no room is left for philosophical speculation. But all of Creation is a work of divine freedom, just as are the redemption and the conferral of grace upon man. Of all this, therefore, we cannot in the least say that it "must" be "so" or "otherwise"—or that it must be "at all." It is useless to wish to search out the "reasons" why God created anything at all and why He created this and not something else instead. It is not valid to assume that the Prime Cause must of necessity cause things. Duns Scotus[10] calls this merely an opinion of the philosophers. According to Christian faith, he argues, it is an attribute of the divine nature to work freely.

Whether and in what sense Duns Scotus was a "voluntarist" has been long debated. The question can of course be decided only if we are clear about the connotations of this epithet. Anyone who calls "voluntaristic" the thesis that the "outwardly directed" working of the divine will is absolutely free must apply the word to all of Christian sacred doctrine. "Voluntarism" in the stricter sense implies two things: an opinion and an attitude. As opinion, we have the ultimate ground of reality being viewed as an absolutely groundless will. "Arbitrary" is almost too mild a term for this will, which is conceived as being completely unconditioned by "grounds" in the sense of reasons. "Voluntarism" as an attitude might be described by the phrase: "delight in blind dynamics." In any such sense, however, Duns Scotus was clearly *not* a "voluntarist." Nevertheless, it seems to me not at all a matter of chance that this appellation has repeatedly been attached to him.

To understand this, we need only consider the concept of "radical spontaneity" which Duns Scotus attributed to all will, both divine and human.[11] Let us think this through to its logical end. An impulse is "spontaneous" which does not come from elsewhere, but only from itself, which sets itself in motion. And undoubtedly there is good sense in maintaining that impulses of the will have this quality; it obviously belongs to the nature of willing that one cannot be made to will from outside. But then, what is the meaning of "from outside"? Is the moving cause, the motive, the act of the intellect which impels one to will, in itself already a limitation upon the spontaneity and freedom of volition? Duns Scotus in fact appears to maintain this when he says that the volition of the will is determined by nothing else than the will itself.[12] In this sense, he holds that being "free" is more essential to the will than its wanting, seeking, desiring "something."[13] If, therefore, "freedom" and "spontaneity" of volition are thus equated with its "groundlessness" (and it is not accidental that "ground" means *raison, reason, ratio*),—then at this point we must ask, Does this not verge, at least as an intellectual possibility, on that type of "voluntarism" which implies blind, purely actual discharge of energy?

But we need pursue this matter no further.

Of more importance, it seems to me, is the question of what becomes of the conjunction of faith and reason as soon as we consider it under this aspect, which Duns Scotus formulated with such decisiveness. If everything that our natural cognition encounters is characterized by *not* being meaningful and necessary in itself; and if above all what faith tells us about God's work of redemption and grace can in no way be made intelligible to reason—*because* all this has no other grounds than the groundless, absolute freedom of God Himself—then what good is there in attempting to co-ordinate faith with speculative reason? How can the two ever meet if reason cannot even set out on the way to faith? What meaning could even the mere concept of "conjunction" continue to have? Does not the scope of speculative reason appear to have been extremely reduced, not only in itself, but especially in its relationship to the truths of faith? Does it not appear to have shrunk to virtually nothing? Let us look closer into this matter.

As a "test case" we may use the question, examined many times since Augustine, of whether God would have become man even if man had not sinned. It is at once clear what seductive opportunities for metaphysical speculation are thrown open by this question to the reasoning intellect, accustomed as it is to thinking in universal interrelationships. I shall adduce only the idea frequently discussed by the scholastics: "There cannot be completion unless the last join with the first. . . . Now since God Himself is the first, and man the last among created beings, it would more accord with the completion of the universe if God had become man even though man had not sinned."[14] Or, we might say, it would be foolish, after all, to assume that man had reaped an advantage by his sinning,[15] or that human nature only through sin became capable of being joined to divine nature to form a unity[16]—and so forth. No one who agrees with the premise of absolute divine freedom as formulated by Duns Scotus can give or even accede to such answers—this much is clear. Rather, he must respond, "In this question the truth can be known solely by Him who was born and 'was offered because it was His own will' (Isaiah 53, 7). That is, those things which depend solely upon the divine will are unknown to us unless they have been made known to us by the authority of the saints to whom God revealed His will." "There is no rational argument for those things that belong to faith"; *ad ea, quae fidei sunt, ratio demonstrativa haberi non potest.*

That is a stout-hearted and clear answer, whose validity we can immediately grant, the more so since it links the idea of incomprehensible divine freedom with the resolutely expressed principle of a primarily *Biblical* theology.

At this point, however, I must confess that although this answer might very well be found in Duns Scotus, it is in reality not his but—Thomas Aquinas'.[17] Two reasons can be advanced in justification of this little deception.

In the first place, I am concerned to show that in this

very fundamental matter Thomas and Duns Scotus held quite the same opinion. It is therefore somewhat misleading to say that by his philosophy—which is "more critical because his theology is more Biblical"—Duns Scotus had corrected the "rational optimism of a St. Thomas."[18]

In the second place, I wish to make it plain that so superior a mind as Thomas Aquinas' could without difficulty expressly acknowledge the principle formulated by Duns Scotus, and nevertheless in no way renounce the attempt to conjoin what he believed with what he knew. For this fact remains: Thomas and Duns Scotus held radically different views of the reciprocal relationship of *fides* and *ratio*—although both agreed that human reason may never touch upon the secret of divine freedom in which are to be found the ground and origin both of Creation and of everything that faith calls redemption and blessing. The question must therefore be raised: In what sense are we to understand Duns Scotus' far more negative, as compared with Thomas', estimate of the possibilities for the conjunction of faith and reason?

To begin with, we must observe that Duns Scotus received his intellectual education at a time in which rationalism had already brought *ratio* irreparably into ill repute, and the "honeymoon of philosophy and theology" had come to a sudden end. Gilson says that even without knowledge of the historical dates "we could guess that the doctrine of Duns Scotus was conceived after the condemnation of 1277"[19]; and that the "Carthage" he had in mind to destroy was "Greek necessitarianism."[20]

But it was not only the atmosphere of the Franciscan school which dominated the field immediately, "the day after"[21] the event of 1277—rather, it was also the mathematical and scientific spirit of Oxford University which had formed Duns Scotus. In Oxford it was customary to demand very high standards of a formal argument which was supposed to prove something. And it appears that Duns Scotus himself contributed a good deal to the sharpening and more precise definition of these standards. That accounts for the critical and aggressive tone in which he couched his disputes with other scholastics, who were less strict in this regard. And it may also explain the tortuous exactitude of his own style; the epithet *doctor subtilis* was a reference to this also. . . . Duns Scotus, we may say, was the first to present that paradoxical dichotomy which became virtually a model for the period following him. I mean: on the one hand to demand an argument so absolutely evident as to be almost beyond human powers, while on the other hand to preach a resignation almost equivalent to renunciation when it came to making "reasons" intelligible.

All this seems almost sufficient in itself to reduce considerably the potentialities of speculative reason. Thomas, for his part, would likewise have welcomed the achievement of greater exactitude in the methods of proof; but he would have warned that absolute certainty is possible only for the absolute spirit, and that there can be many intermediary phases between the greatest possible evidence and the absolute impossibility of understanding. Thus, hard upon the statement that there can be no rational proof in matters of faith, we find a further statement that it is nevertheless possible not only to prove that the Incarnation (for example) is not an absurd and self-contradictory idea, but also that it is meaningful (*congruens*) in itself.[22] Obviously this means that the potentialities of natural reason in its relationship to faith are by no means meager.

Yet Duns Scotus set small store upon these potentialities

of reason even in its most proper sphere—not, of course, because he himself was agnostic, nor solely because he had raised the standard of the formal requirements for proof so high, but once again on the basis of his *theological* principle. What essentially took place here is difficult to grasp. One way of putting it is to say that Duns Scotus was by-passing the reality of natural creation itself, and *thereby* taking away the certainty of man's cognition of it. When, for example, he stated that the immortality of the soul cannot be proved by rational arguments, he was speaking partly in terms of his own high standards of proof—standards which can be met only by mathematics. And in this respect his criticism of the well-known philosophical arguments was extremely keen. Yet his own thesis would be not only that the immortality of the soul has not hitherto been adequately proved, but that it is in principle unprovable—because the soul itself has proceeded, as something nonnecessary, from the freedom of God and therefore may as easily be restored to nothingness by God.[23] Wherewith the circle closes—on Duns Scotus' watchword: freedom.

To the retrospective eye a strange phenomenon is revealed: that Duns Scotus' theological starting point has made the conjunction of the believed with the known every bit as difficult a matter as Siger of Brabant's secularistic-philosophical point of view. "Double truth" comes to the fore again as a danger threatening from *both* sides. And by that very fact we see that the pair, Siger of Brabant and Duns Scotus, stood on the outer border of the age to which Boethius, Anselm, Abélard and Thomas Aquinas belonged fully, different as these men were from one another.

The step out of the Middle Ages was not to be taken until the next generation—by *William of Ockham*. His dramatic biography has already been briefly touched on. Born in the vicinity of London around 1298, this brilliant Franciscan became a teacher at Oxford by the time he was twenty. But in 1324, even before he had attained the degree of *magister*, he was summoned to appear before the Papal See at Avignon to answer charges of unorthodox doctrines. This spelled the end of his career as teacher, and indeed of his career as philosopher and theologian. All his works in these two fields which have come down to us (including a systematic logic, an elucidation of Aristotle's *Physics,* and an uncompleted commentary on the *Sentences*) were written before this time. He fled from Avignon, accompanied by Michael of Cesena, minister general of the Franciscan Order, who was later expelled from that order. The two men took refuge at the court of the German Emperor, Louis of Bavaria, and William at once threw himself into passionate pamphleteering in the dispute between Emperor and Pope—fighting by the side of another refugee whom he found already in Munich: Marsilius of Padua, whose antipapal memorial, *Defensor Pacis,* called for the Church to withdraw from secular things. After the Emperor's death (1347) William of Ockham appears to have made a reconciliation with the Church. Two years later he fell victim to the plague in Munich.

Although Duns Scotus was such a universal spirit that it is impossible to regard him as a mere "forerunner" of William of Ockham; and although William, young revolutionary that he was, specifically declared his opposition to Duns Scotus, whom he regarded as already "belonging to the ancients"[24] (because he "tried to prove too much"[25])—William nevertheless led the way along the very same path upon which Duns Scotus had first set foot. William of Ockham's doctrine, too, can be regarded as a reaction, pushed further and further, to the "Averroism" of the theses condemned in 1277.[26] Above all, he too laid stress on the principle of absolute divine freedom, which was to be understood primarily as unlimited freedom in the exercise of power. "As God creates every creature merely because He wishes it, so He can also do whatever He pleases with that creature"; He could "without injustice annihilate" a man living wholly according to God's will.[27] The excessiveness of this kind of thinking comes to light in the almost brutal way in which William of Ockham envisages the various alternatives to the story of man's redemption. He argues that God's becoming man, for example, was so little meaningful and necessary "in itself" that God, if He had wished, might just as well have assumed the nature of a stone, a tree, or an ass.[28]

Although such a statement seems to emphasize to the extreme man's incapacity to know anything, it is in fact far more assertive and "imperious" than, say, the statement of Thomas Aquinas, who does not speak of stones or asses or other bizarre alternatives. Rather, considering faith's tenet that God became *man,* he simply says that we would know *nothing at all* if it had not been revealed to us. And even though Thomas proceeds to try to make the fact of the Incarnation intelligible as something meaningful and "congruent" in itself, his attitude contains far more of silent respect for the mystery than William of Ockham's wordy proclamation of God's "otherness." The same may be said for the disciplined discretion with which Thomas speaks of the possibility—one that he also takes for granted—that *si Deo placeret*[29] all things could sink back into nothingness. To him, the fact of creation itself is the expression of the free divine will.[30] He cites Scripture in support of this: " 'God has created all things that they may be' [Wisdom 1, 14], not that they may sink back into nothingness."[31] But William of Ockham, again going to the extreme, derives from the principle of God's arbitrary freedom a conclusion fraught with the gravest consequences. This conclusion may be summarized as follows: Man cannot do anything but cling to the purely factual, which in no way must be as it is; to search for meaning and coherence is vain; the coherence is not "real," but at most may exist in our thoughts; singular facts alone are "real"; this actual factuality, however, can neither be calculated nor investigated nor deduced, but only *experienced*; knowledge exists only as direct encounter with concrete reality.

The consequences of these ideas for the practice of philosophy are self-evident. Nevertheless, let us remember that the root from which this empiricism springs is a theological one. And the type of theology which alone can thrive upon such soil scarcely needs to be defined more specifically; it can only be a purely "positive" theology which rejects as untheological any possibility of collaboration with speculative reason.

This violent reaction to the style of philosophical and theological thought in the preceding era was, however, something inevitable. For one thing, after the tremendous intellectual effort of the century of the *Summae,* a certain weariness, a lack of energy for putting ideas in order, and probably a certain impatience with the system-building efforts of speculative philosophy, were only to be expected. A generation after William of Ockham, the author of a commentary on the *Sentences,* Petrus of Candia (a Greek from Crete, *magister* of the University of Paris, later Archbishop of Milan, and finally Pope Alexander V), would think nothing of setting down side by side, with brash unconcern for any sequence, theses utterly incompatible with one another; his explanation was that he was doing this "for the convenience of those who desire to eat sometimes bread and sometimes cheese."[32]

Above all else it was the entrancing wealth of the natural world, now becoming accessible in all its limitless variety, that inspired this empiricism, this turning to concrete reality. And who would deny that scholastic theology was in vital need of "isolation," that it needed to retreat for a time into its most interior cell in order to contemplate, without distraction, that "divine speech" whose interpretation was its true, its sole task.

Nevertheless, in this period represented by the name of William of Ockham, extremely dangerous processes were being set in motion, and many a future trouble was preparing. On that question, to be sure, opinions will always vary in regard to detail.

But one thing is undeniable, and indeed has not been denied: Just as in the political realm the form of Christianity which had been developed since the end of antiquity, and which had been founded on the special accord between the spiritual and secular powers, was beginning to break down, so also in the realm of the mind—starting at the very moment that the era reached its apex—a progressive divergence between faith and reason was taking place. Inexorably, and justified by reasons on both sides, divorce was taking place between *fides* and *ratio*—to whose conjunction the energies of almost a thousand years had been devoted. What was taking place, in short, was the end of the Middle Ages.

XII

It is not only the era "between" antiquity and modern times but also modern times, so called, that are at an end. Whoever desires to learn not "how things used to be," but rather how things stand here and now with the matters which have always been and will always be worth thinking about—the philosophically minded person, that is, who looks across the span of a whole epoch at the Middle Ages and its philosophy—that person asks about the contemporaneity of the Middle Ages.

We are not proposing an inquiry into the "survival" of medieval concepts and notions in present-day thinking. Such survivals are always cropping up, in a thousand different ways, and frequently go entirely unnoticed; the pasts of all epochs and all regions of the world, and thus also of the Middle Ages, are always present and continuously operative in some fashion. This is one of the basic phenomena of mankind's history. We hear, for example: "If the eye had nought of the sun,/How could we ever behold the light . . ." and we say: Goethe. Goethe himself, however, says: "An ancient mystic." From which we learn that these wholly Goethean verses are an attempt to express an idea of Plotinus'[1] "in German rhymes."[2] Such continuity of the past wins through, continues to operate, even when the past is deliberately rejected. Sartre's drama No Exit, for example, is inconceivable without the "medieval" conception of hell. When we speak, therefore, of the possible contemporaneity of the Middle Ages, we are not out to uncover relationships of this sort.

Neither are we referring to the subject of medieval philosophy with which, not surprisingly, the philosophy of all ages has dealt. Rather, we are concerned with those structural elements of medieval philosophizing which we have discovered to be "specifically medieval," and which we might imagine would have fallen into disuse and opprobrium with the end of that era itself. We wonder whether this seemingly "medieval" matter may not have a special contemporaneity, whether it may not be highly relevant to the present-day practitioner of philosophy.

The picture of medieval philosophy is composed, as we have seen, out of the following elements: The young peoples of the North and West of Europe undertook by methodical study to acquire and assimilate pagan and Christian antiquity's stock of tradition. The sheltered preserve in which the intellectual life of the period was able to function was the area of the Church (monastery, cathedral school, papal-sponsored university). The practice of philosophy, in which for the most part only monks and clerics engaged, started out from theological questions and with theological aims. In this very special sense it was "Christian philosophy." Given all these factors, does it not seem improbable that there should be anything contemporary about the philosophy of the Middle Ages?

Let us begin, then, with what seems most improbable. Obviously, the situation in which tradition was assimilated by the mere process of learning is a thing of the past. The attempt to arrest the flux of thought by strict enforcement of the teachings of authority—in times when men's direct experience with the world was bringing in a host of new discoveries, whose vitality far surpassed that of the old material[3]—precisely this spelled the end of the Middle Ages. There can be no disagreement on this point.

Nevertheless, a word must be said here concerning the experiment with the "Great Books" which has been undertaken at American centers of learning. Here is a curriculum based on certain books which represent the cultural "heritage": their authors are Homer, Plato, Aristotle, Virgil, Plotinus, Augustine, St. Thomas, Dante, Shakespeare, Kant, Hegel, Goethe, Darwin, Dostoevsky, and Sigmund Freud. It is possible to quarrel with this or that aspect of the project. Nevertheless this attempt,[4] carried out with the earnestness of great open-mindedness, sprang from a conviction that the young continent could come into possession of its rightful intellectual inheritance only if that inheritance were made teachable and learnable in this fashion. This is not so very different from the impulse and necessity which produced the schoolmasterly enterprise of medieval scholasticism. And not only the problems but the "problematic," which is to say the dubious, aspects of the matter are largely identical. Thus, there is the question of translation (in the broadest sense)—unavoidable under the circumstances, but nevertheless posing its own special difficulties. There is the question of the selection of the material, and the inevitable omissions. There is the question of how much simplification is legitimate, and where it is going too far. The possibly too facile determination to take the questionable aspects into the bargain, in the face of the simple vital necessity, likewise seems much the same.

It might be argued, to be sure, that while this is not

uninteresting, the parallel is at bottom little more than a matter of chance. I think otherwise. Through such a program those American students who may be "majoring" in other subjects do, after all, become acquainted more or less at first hand, though in translation, with both the *Nichomachean Ethics* and the *Meditations* of Marcus Aurelius, with large parts of St. Thomas' *Summa theologica* and with Pascal's *Pensées*. And when one comes in contact with these students, one is aware of a perceptible difference. Returning to our European universities, one feels clearly that such "scholasticism" would profit us as well. It offers one of the very few possibilities of keeping at all recognizable and present to the minds of the young the "fund of wisdom" on which man lives spiritually. That fund, that heritage, or whatever we may choose to call it, has grown so huge—by a natural process, not at all because it has been wantonly accumulated—that its entirety can no longer be commanded by anyone.

A further question must be posed here. There is still another stock of tradition which has become accessible to us, first as "conquerors," too. I am speaking of the non-European, above all the Far Eastern, cultures. Can this vast wealth of knowledge of man and of philosophical interpretation of reality be assimilated—if at all—in any other than a "scholastic" manner? Hitherto scarcely any such attempt has been made, except by specialists. No doubt there are many reasons for that. Might not one of these reasons be, however, that we have lost our hold on the technique of "learning"? Still another reason may be that, before such assimilation is undertaken, there must first be the insight that there is a task here, one beyond mere historical observation: a task which carries its own obligation and offers its own reward. Perhaps that insight is granted only to one who is capable of seeing truth in the world, wherever he encounters it, as part of the One Divine Logos.

Let us consider the second feature of medieval scholasticism—its setting within the area of the Church. That, above all, seems clearly over and done with. And in fact it was a symbolic event when William of Ockham fled from the Minorite cloister to the German imperial court. For he was traversing the same path, but in a reverse direction, as was traversed at the beginning of the epoch by Cassiodorus when he abandoned his political office at the court of the Gothic king and retired to the cloister. From William of Ockham's time on, then, philosophy once more took up its residence in the larger "breathing space" of the "world." Today we can scarcely imagine any other state of affairs.

And yet—do we not find ourselves somewhat caught in the modern world of work—faced with the increasing politicalization of the academic realm and the ominous shrinking of inner and outer opportunities for public discourse, and especially for genuine debate? Where shall we seek the "free area" in which alone *theoria* can thrive (and by *theoria* we mean concern, limited by no practical [political, economic, technical, sectarian] considerations, with "truth and nothing else")? We begin to understand that Plato's Academy had been a *thiasos,* a religious association assembling for regular sacrificial worship. Does this have any bearing on our own time?

The question, which medieval philosophy answered by entering into the four walls of the monastery, within which, nota bene, was room not only for the Bible and the Church Fathers, but also for Plato, Aristotle, Cicero,

Seneca and the great Arabs—this question must evidently be answered anew in every period. I find it indicative of the difficulty of a modern answer that a man like T. S. Eliot[5] should declare straight out: a strengthening of monastic life is desirable today, so that within the sheltered preserve of the cloister, "uncontaminated by the deluge of barbarism outside," a certain number of people may receive a philosophical education which will be "something more than education for a place in the Civil Service, or for technical efficiency, or for social or public success." This seems to me to be a thoroughly utopian proposal— and presumably its author has no illusions about that. Still, what more "modern" solution offers itself to this problem? And would not this solution be objectively effective? On these grounds, we may perhaps agree with T. S. Eliot that the medieval solution is less "medieval" than it would at first sight seem to be.

We come to the last-named and no longer purely formal structural element: that medieval philosophy was a "Christian philosophy," not only practiced by monks and clerics, but also determined in its subject matter by theology. Here we are dealing with a rather difficult problem, but also with the crucial one.

The subject has two branches: the structure of Christian philosophy in general, and the precedence of theological questions within this structure. Let us consider these things in terms of the "contemporaneity of the Middle Ages."

To examine the framework of "Christian philosophy," we must first accept a basic premise. This is the premise that in Christ man received an intelligence which relates to the whole of the universe and of existence, and therefore by definition concerns anyone who engages in philosophizing—and which, moreover, is valid by virtue of a superhuman claim to truth.

Should anyone reject this premise, he must in consistency regard "Christian philosophy," however one defines it, as meaningless. The whole of medieval philosophy must remain inaccessible to him, as far as its sole underlying motif is concerned. It cannot help but strike him as a perhaps amazing but in the final analysis senseless expenditure of formalistic ingenuity—even though he may recognize it as ever so comprehensible "historically" and even though he may pay it tribute for certain advances in logic, say, in the interpretation of Aristotle, or in other matters.

On the other hand, suppose that the premise is granted. Then the task of "conjunction" comes to the fore—the question, at least, in what way the *believed* intelligence concerning the world and existence can be made to accord with the *known* intelligence concerning that same world and that same human existence as it is revealed to men's eyes. If man is desirous of existing out of the fullness and out of the unchecked energies of the spiritual impulse—which means existing in the face of absolutely everything that comes within his scope—then he is bound at least to attempt the conjunction of *fides* and *ratio*. Granted the premise that he accepts both, what is believed and what is known, as true, that is to say, as offering real intelligence concerning reality—then this is a task which cannot be evaded.

The conjunction of *fides* and *ratio* involves two operations: first, the *interpretation* of the divine message as it greets man in the shape of image, symbol, and event, and also in the lineaments of a particular culture. To be binding or even merely credible, this interpretation, which is the real business of theology, must bring into play the total body of truth known to man. The second operation would be to bring this interpretation into accord with the whole of natural knowledge of the world and existence.[6]

As our review of the period has shown, this was the supreme theme of philosophical and theological efforts between Boethius and Duns Scotus. Certain efforts toward a solution proved to be, even during the Middle Ages themselves, unrealizable. But for the Christian engaged in philosophy today, the great attempts have not lost their validity as paradigms. By this we mean that these were realizations which we must cherish, despite the fact that they cannot be simply imitated or repeated. They are thus partly "contemporary" and partly "outmoded."

Outmoded beyond recall, it would seem, are the *Summae*. To be sure, even Thomas Aquinas spoke of the unfathomableness of all reality. Nevertheless his attitude strikes us as that of a man who surveys a bright room full of immeasurable but nevertheless well-ordered treasures; whereas our relationship to the world is rather that of a man let down into the depths of the sea in a bathysphere, who knows himself surrounded by mysteries, by illimitable darkness, and is able to discern only what lies within the range of his searchlight. For us, there is no longer any attaining of a closed and rounded view of the world, in any legitimate way. The wealth of available knowledge of the natural world has become too boundless. Nor would it do for either the scientist, the philosopher, or the theologian to attempt to create a premature unity out of multiplicity by the mere addition of a "Christian aspect."

Yet herein lies the peculiarly modern task. By relinquishing any attempt to close off the image of reality, by deliberately practicing an openness of vision—theology toward science and science toward theology (not on the basis of any special act of reverence, but on the basis of a disciplined perception of how little is as yet actually knowable), but also by letting theology participate in the ever-advancing investigation of the world and of man or, to use a word from theological terminology: of creation— by this explicit renunciation the image of the fundamentally unitary world might be saved and the view of the Whole kept free from all obstructions.

Here is the point to recall that the greatest *Summa* of the Middle Ages not only remained uncompleted—not just by chance, but because its author, Thomas Aquinas, wished it so—but also that it was meant as an elementary textbook "for the instruction of beginners"—*ad eruditionem incipientium*.[7] Which means that even had it been completed it would not have pretended to ultimate conclusiveness. The "ultimate" Thomas is rather to be found in his *Quaestiones disputatae.* The title can be rendered as "Questions examined in the course of debate." The *Quaestiones* were the fruit of that type of discussion whose guiding principle is not so much to overcome the opponent or to reach any "conclusion" as mutually to explore a question as far as possible, to carve a path to knowledge opening out to infinity. One might well say that the universality of the High Middle Ages was achieved less in the individual performances of the great *Summae* than in this *recherche collective de la vérité*,[8] that is, in the "disputations" which barred no subject and no partner to the debate. None at all, not even the non-Christians! There is the mistaken idea that medieval philosophy was

an "internal Christian" affair limited to a circle of inti-
mates and initiates. To be sure, one of the ground rules
of medieval disputation was that a debate on things whose
fundaments were not acknowledged by all the partners
would be impossible and hopeless. But Thomas cites one
fundament which is recognized by everyone and which
made it possible to debate even with "Mohammedans and
pagans": "natural reason."[9] And he himself led this
debate—in the wholly unpolemical book later so wrongly
entitled *Summa against the Pagans.* "Natural reason,"
however, as he meant it, is not primarily the dialectic
adroitness to vanquish another in debate, but rather the
strength to "listen to" everything one encounters.

It should be fairly clear that such an exemplary style
of conjoining faith and reason would be eminently suit-
able for our own time.

We have still to speak of the role assigned to theology
in the medieval approach to the problem of *fides* and
ratio. Theology was of course given precedence. Here,
too, we can find certain elements which are irrevocably
outmoded, and certain others which remain valid. The
contributions that the Middle Ages made to philosophical
knowledge do have a purely philosophical character.
Thomas, countering the usual theological scruples, firmly
defended the right of philosophy to investigate any subject
under the sun[10] (supporting this by theological arguments). Nevertheless, the fact remains that all these
philosophers were simultaneously theologians. What is
more, their philosophizing, as was only to be expected,
began with an impulse to ask theological questions. This
impulse is obviously entirely outmoded. The very contrary obtains. The living practice of philosophy at the

present time springs precisely from what is not theology, springs rather from the historical experiences of the times, from modern physics, from depth psychology, from evolutionary research.

Nevertheless, two things must be considered. First: As long as the believed message upon which Christian philosophizing is ultimately based continues to be regarded as "divine speech," as "revelation" in the strict sense of the word, it will *eo ipso* also be understood as an absolutely superordinate standard of truth. However we may cast this matter of superordination and subordination, it is part and parcel of the notion of a "Christian philosophy" that natural reason takes on an inferior meaning in relation to God's revelation. Naturally, it is a great question whether such a limitation upon the autonomy of reason is defensible or not. We must realize, however, that this discussion centers not around the distinction between "medieval" and "modern," but around the distinction between "Christian" and "non-Christian."

Second: When we bring natural knowledge into the more comprehensive truth of revelation, we for the first time see the true illuminatory power of scientific and philosophical discoveries—assuming that we make this synthesis *legitimately,* that is to say, upon the basis of a good and accurate knowledge both of theological and of natural truth. "Mysticism is . . . the only power which is capable of uniting in a synthesis the riches accumulated by other forms of human activity." This sentence was written by Pierre Teilhard de Chardin,[11] one of the boldest and most spiritual of the theological thinkers of our time, who is at the same time an outstanding figure in paleontological research. No one can fail to be impressed by the *élan* with which Teilhard de Chardin combines his vision of a "greater Christ"[12] with the discoveries of evolutionary theory. We begin to see how remarkably a conjunction of *fides* and *ratio* inspired by theology—in so far as that conjunction is arrived at with entire legitimacy—can release the powers of natural reason to the full, allowing it the widest scope to achieve knowledge of our world.

"Christian philosophy" is not a more or less abstruse brand of philosophical activity corresponding to the special ("religious") interests of individuals. It is *the* only possible form of philosophy[13]—*if* it is true that the *Logos* of God became man in Christ, and *if* by "philosophy" we understand what the great forefathers of European philosophizing (Pythagoras, Plato, Aristotle) meant by it. The thinkers of the Middle Ages perceived that a "Christian philosophy" depended upon the conjunction of *fides* and *ratio*. This was the task they set themselves, and into this task they poured their full intellectual resources. This task is continuous and never-ending. Anyone who addresses himself today to this same task cannot afford to ignore the demanding and multiform paradigm of medieval philosophy. But in answer to the questions posed he cannot take the medieval view; he will have to find his own answer.

WORKS OF REFERENCE
NOTES
CHRONOLOGICAL TABLE
INDEX

Bernhard Geyer, *Die patristische und scholastische Philosophie.* 11th edition, Berlin, 1928. This book, the second volume of *"Friedrich Überwegs Grundriss der Geschichte der Philosophie,"* remains indispensable, despite the fact that many of its details are superseded.   Cited as: Überweg-Geyer

☆

Étienne Gilson, *History of Christian Philosophy in the Middle Ages.* London and New York, 1955. A masterly, comprehensive treatment, as thorough as it is readable.

Cited as: Gilson, *History*

☆

Philotheus Böhner and Étienne Gilson, *Christliche Philosophie von ihren Anfängen bis Nikolaus von Cues.* 3rd edition, Paderborn, 1954. Not a translation of the *History*, but a completely different book in arrangement and content. Though Gilson is given as co-author, this book is largely the work of Böhner.   Cited as: Böhner, *Christl. Philosophie*

☆

Maurice de Wulf, *Histoire de la philosophie médiévale.* 6th edition. Three volumes, Louvain, 1934, 1936, 1947. The long out-of-print first volume of this edition is also available in English translation (London, 1951).

Cited as: de Wulf, *Histoire*

☆

Frederick Copleston, *Mediaeval Philosophy. Augustine to Scotus.* (Volume II of *A History of Philosophy*.) London, 1950. Very clear. Rich in quotations.   Cited as: Copleston

☆

The well-planned 13th volume of the *Histoire de l'Église* by Fliche-Martin, entitled *Le mouvement doctrinal du XIe au XIVe siècle* (Paris, 1951), includes three large sections:

(1) André Forest, *De Jean Scot Érigène au siècle des universités* Cited as: Forest, *De Jean Scot Érigène*

(2) Fernand van Steenberghen, *Le XIIIe siècle.*
  Cited as: van Steenberghen, *Le XIIIe siècle*

(3) M. de Gandillac, *Le XIVe siècle.*

☆

Albert Stöckl, *Geschichte der Philosophie des Mittelalters.* Three volumes, Mainz, 1864-66. Still valuable because of the numerous texts and clear judgments, although the latter are in many respects now superseded.

☆

Martin Grabmann, *Die Geschichte der scholastischen Methode.* Two volumes, Freiburg, 1909, 1911; reprint, Darmstadt, 1956.
  Cited as: Grabmann, *Scholast. Methode*

☆

Martin Grabmann, *Mittelalterliches Geistesleben.* Three volumes, Munich, 1926, 1936, 1956. This work, although a collection of monographs, serves as an excellent general survey.
  Cited as: Grabmann, *Mittelalterl. Geistesleben*

☆

Fernand van Steenberghen, *Philosophie des Mittelalters.* Bern, 1950. A brief, purely bibliographical introduction.

The motto is to be found in a letter (or draft of one) to Heinrich Jung-Stilling, written in the spring of 1789.

Preface

[1] Josef Pieper, *Hinführung zu Thomas von Aquin. Zwölf Vorlesungen.* Munich (Kösel Verlag), 1958. English edition in preparation.

I

[1] G. Gordon, *Medium Aevum and the Middle Age.* Oxford, 1925.
[2] Hegel, *Sämtliche Werke* (Jubiläumsausgabe). Ed. H. Glockner. Vol. 19 (Stuttgart, 1928), p. 99.
[3] Ibid., p. 328.
[4] Ibid., p. 149. Alongside of secondary works and compendia, the only source book Hegel mentions is St. Thomas' *Summa theologica.* This might well redound to his credit, were it not to be feared that by the "terribly written and voluminous" works he was referring to this very book.
[5] Some particularly important names: Cl. Baeumker, Fr. Ehrle, B. Geyer, M. Grabmann, J. Koch, A. Landgraf, A. Stöckl, M.-D. Chenu, É. Gilson, P. Mandonnet, J. Maritain, F. van Steenberghen, M. de Wulf. Here we should also mention the treatise by J. Erdmann, which, in spite of a number of odd judgments on individual points, is an amazingly acute work for its period: *"Der Entwicklungsgang der Scholastik"* (*Zeitschrift für wissenschaftliche Theologie*, 8. Jahrgang [Halle, 1865], pp. 113-71).
[6] Hegel, loc. cit., p. 99.
[7] K. Jaspers, *Vom Ursprung und Ziel der Geschichte.* Munich, 1949, p. 19.
[8] Ibid., pp. 19 f.
[9] Gilson, *History,* pp. 3 f.
[10] Hegel, loc. cit., p. 139.

[11] Ibid., p. 199.
[12] Ibid., p. 201.
[13] *Scholast. Methode* I, p. 137.
[14] *History,* p. 528.
[15] This applies to the fourth edition (Louvain, 1912), translated into German by R. Eisler: M. de Wulf, *Geschichte der mittelalterlichen Philosophie* (Tübingen, 1913), p. 448.

II

[1] Cf. on this M. L. Gothein, *Nachwort* to the Latin-German edition of the *Consolatio,* translated by Eberhard Gothein (Berlin, 1932), pp. 195, 205.
[2] Böhner, *Christl. Philosophie,* p. 247.
[3] Commentary on *Peri hermeneias,* second version Migne, *Patrologia Latina* 64, 433.
[4] . . . *In plerisque quae sunt in philosophia maxime consentire.* Ibid.
[5] First poem in the *Consolatio.*
[6] "His textbook on Music, founded upon various Greek authorities, was in use at Oxford and Cambridge until modern times." E. K. Rand in: Boethius, *Theological tractates* etc., Loeb Classical Library (1953), p. X.
[7] Cf. Grabmann, *Die theologische Erkenntnis- und Einleitungslehre des heiligen Thomas von Aquin.* (Freiburg, 1948), p. 3.
[8] *Consolatio* V, 6 prosa.
[9] Ibid., V, 4 prosa.
[10] It has been asserted (by Fr. Heer, *Europäische Geistesgeschichte* [1953], p. 33) that aside from the Bible and the *Imitation of Christ* no book in world history has been so frequently copied, translated, commented on, and printed. However that may be, there exist today—from the period before the invention of printing—more than 400 manuscripts of the *Consolatio,* and within a bare fifty years after the Gutenberg Bible it was printed 43 times. Notker Labeo translated it into German, Alfred the Great into Anglo-Saxon, and Chaucer

into English. There are medieval translations into French, Greek, Spanish, and Hebrew.

[11] *Consolatio* II, 4 prosa.

[12] Ibid., II, 5 prosa.

[13] Cf. Josef Pieper, *Erkenntnis und Freiheit*. In: *Weistum, Dichtung, Sakrament* (Munich, 1954), p. 40.

[14] *Consolatio* V, 2 prosa.

[15] Ibid., I, 4 prosa.

[16] Ibid., III, 12 prosa.

[17] Ibid., V, 3 prosa.

[18] E. K. Rand, *Founders of the Middle Ages* (Cambridge, Mass., 1928), pp. 135 ff.

[19] Grabmann, *Scholast. Methode* I, p. 148.

[20] Boethius, *Theological tractates,* etc. Loeb Classical Library (1953), p. X: "The theological tractates mark him as the forerunner of St. Thomas."

[21] Grabmann, *Theol. Erkenntnis- und Einleitungslehre*, p. 5.

[22] Gilson, *History*, p. 106.

[23] At the time he wrote his magnificent prologue to his commentary on Boethius' tractate on the Trinity, Thomas Aquinas used "a great number of Scriptural passages, but not a single quotation from Aristotle." Cf. Grabmann, *Theolog. Erkenntnis- und Einleitungslehre*, p. 37.

[24] Commentary on the Sentences 1 d. 2, divisio textus.

[25] G. Schnürer, *Die Anfänge der abendländischen Völkergemeinschaft* (Freiburg, 1932), pp. 82, 88.

[26] Cassiodorus wrote both a *Chronicle* (around 519) and a *History of the Goths* (between 526 and 533).

[27] To be sure, the monastic "free area" remained inviolable because the secular powers respected it. Amid the chaos of the sixth century, however, this may be rightly said. An emissary of the (Arian) Goth Witigis told the Eastern Roman general Belisarius: "We have always held the sanctuaries of the Romans in the highest honor; never has anyone who sought refuge there had so much as a hair of his head harmed."

(Procopius, *Gothic War*, II, 6.) This statement is altogether worthy of credence.

[28] J. A. Möhler, *Gesammelte Schriften und Aufsätze*. Ed. by I. Döllinger (Regensburg, 1839), II, pp. 35 f.
[29] *Institutiones* II, 3.

III

[1] Cf. Josef Pieper, *Zucht und Mass* (Kösel Verlag, Munich, 8th ed., 1960), pp. 30 ff. English translation, *Fortitude and Temperance* (London and New York, 1954).
[2] Cf. Chap. IV (pp. 61 ff.) and Chap. XI (pp. 136 ff.).
[3] This is the name usually given in historical literature. For simplicity's sake we will speak of Dionysius Areopagita.
[4] Böhner, *Christl. Philosophie*, p. 131.
[5] Thus J. Stiglmayr in the introduction to his translation of the two hierarchies (*Bibliothek der Kirchenväter*, Kempten and Munich, 1911), p. XXIII.
[6] H. F. Müller, *Dionysios, Proklos, Plotinos* (Münster, 1918), p. 110.
[7] Ibid., p. 37.
[8] Ibid., p. 38.
[9] A. Feder, "*Des Aquinaten Kommentar zu Pseudo-Dionysius' De divinis nominibus.*" *Scholastik*, Jahrgang 1 (1926), p. 335.
[10] Thomas, dealing with the duties of the angels in his commentary on the *Sentences* (2 d. 10, 1, 2), says that a particular view is *rationabilior . . . quia Dionysius hoc tradit, qui discipulus Pauli fuit et dicitur ejus visiones scripsisse.*
[11] Böhner, *Christl. Philosophie*, p. 131.
[12] E. Underhill, *Mysticism* (London, 1957).
[13] Ibid.
[14] Cf. Grabmann, *Mittelalterl. Geistesleben* I, p. 450.
[15] M.-D. Chenu, *Introduction à l'étude de St Thomas d'Aquin* (Paris, 1950), p. 193.
[16] *Traité de l'amour de Dieu* I, 9.
[17] De Wulf, *Histoire* (Engl. translation) I, p. 101.
[18] Ibid.

[19] The name Scotus Eriugena (Erigena), as it is quite often given, is tautological, since it expresses the same fact twice: John's origin in Ireland (Scotland as it was called in the Middle Ages). Johannes Scotus or John the Scot makes sense.
[20] The curious fact that the language and documents of dying antiquity were better preserved in the British Isles than elsewhere has several causes. The British Isles were the first mission territory directly converted from Rome. The Irish national saint, the missionary St. Patrick, was a Roman. And one of the first bishops of Canterbury, the founder of the fame of Canterbury—Bishop Theodore (seventh century)—came from the Greek-speaking Tarsus in Asia Minor. He brought with him his Homer, and read it constantly. (G. Schnürer, *Anfänge der abendl. Völkergemeinschaft*, p. 177.) Thus early he introduced classical studies into the English cathedral schools.
[21] Böhner, *Christl. Philosophie*.
[22] Gilson, *History*, p. 113.
[23] Ibid., p. 113.
[24] Böhner speaks of "hierarchy as a task"; *Christl. Philosophie*, pp. 138 f.
[25] *De divinis nominibus* I, §1, 7.
[26] It is quite plain that this idea goes back to Plato. In Plato's *Politeia* (509 b 8 f.) it is stated that the Good, *theion*, is not an entity, but surpasses Being itself in dignity and power. Whereupon Glaucon exclaims in amazement: "By Apollo, what surpassing deviltry" (509 b 9). In Plotinus (*Enn.* VI, 9, 3; in the Greek-German edition of R. Harder [Hamburg, 1956] I, p. 181) the same thought reappears in the following form: "Since . . . the essence of the One is the engenderer of all things, it is one of them. It is, therefore, neither a Something nor a Thus-made nor a So-and-so-much, neither mind nor soul, neither moved nor at rest, neither in space nor in time."
[27] *Serm.* 117, 3; 5—ibid., 52, 6; 16. *In Psalm.* 85, 12—ibid., 99, 5 f. *De doctrina Christiana*, 1, 6; 6. *In Johannem*, tract. 13, 5. *De trinitate* 5, 1; 1. Ibid., 7, 4; 7.

[28] Chenu, Introduction, p. 193.
[29] I, 3 prooem.
[30] Commentary on Boethius, *De trinitate* 2, 1 ad 6.
[31] Ibid., 1, 2 ad 1.
[82] *Quaest. disp. de Potentia Dei* 7, 5 ad 14.
[33] *Celestial Hierarchy* 15, 9. *Mystic Theology,* cap. 1.
[84] Grabmann, *Mittelalterl. Geistesleben* I, p. 466; II, p. 389.

IV

[1] In the fourth homily (on Matt. 17); Migne, *Patrologia Latina* 158, 600 f. Nevertheless, he speaks there of *venerandus Pater Dionysius* and of *beati Dionysii tam ponderosa verba.*
[2] Gilson, *History,* p. 129.
[3] Even the editor of the critical collected edition of Anselm's works (published in England), F. S. Schmitt, O.S.B., says in the introduction to the Latin-German edition of *Cur Deus homo* (Kösel Verlag, Munich, 1956): "It cannot be denied that Anselm went farther than is permissible in his attempt to arrive at a rational comprehension of faith. . . ." (p. VIII).
[4] J. A. Möhler, *Ges. Schriften* I, p. 41.
[5] I, 1, 6.
[6] Ibid.
[7] *Epistolae* 3, nr. 7. Migne, *Patrologia Latina* 159, 24.
[8] II, 4, 34.
[9] Eadmer, *Historia novorum,* lib. II. Migne, *Patrologia Latina* 159, 405 f.
[10] Eadmer, *Vita* II, 1, 8.
[11] II, 3, 29.
[12] *Proslogion,* prooem.
[13] *In Johannem* tract. 40, 9.
[14] Commentary on Boethius, *De trinitate,* prooem.
[15] Grabmann, *Scholast. Methode* I, 259 ff.
[16] Ibid., I, 270.
[17] *. . . quasi nihil sciatur de Christo . . . ; . . . quasi numquam aliquid fuerit de illo. Cur Deus homo,* prooem.
[18] *Cur Deus homo,* I, 16.
[19] Ibid., II, 8.

[20] Ibid., II, 9.

[21] Gilson, *History*, p. 129.

[22] *Sämtl. Werke*, Vol. 19, p. 163.

[23] Commentary on Boethius, *De trinitate* 2, 1 ad 5.

[24] Ibid., 2, 3 ad 5.

[25] F. S. Schmitt, Introduction to the Latin-German edition of *Cur Deus homo*, p. IX.

[26] *Proslogion*, cap. 1. In contrast to the earlier *Monologion*, this is a *new* idea. Some have conjectured that it might have been advanced in defense—addressed, for example, to Lanfranc, who had written to Anselm criticizing the *Monologion* for, among other things, excluding all arguments derived from the Bible. Cf. Adolf Kolping, *Anselms Proslogion-Beweis der Existenz Gottes* (Bonn, 1939), p. 7.

[27] *Cur Deus homo* I, 2.

[28] Ibid.

[29] *Critique of Pure Reason*, ed. by R. Schmidt (Leipzig, 1944), p. 567.

[30] I, 2, 26.

[31] *Proslogion*, prooem.

[32] I, 2, 26.

[33] Migne, printed in *Patrologia Latina* 158, 241 ff.

[34] *Liber Apologeticus contra Gaunilonem*. Migne, *Patrologia Latina* 158, 247 ff.

[35] Apparently neither Anselm nor Eadmer knew the name of the author of this polemic.

[36] K. Barth, *Fides quaerens intellectum* (Munich, 1931).

[37] In addition to the text of the *Proslogion* I am here drawing upon Anselm's reply to Gaunilon.

[38] Cf. *Anselm von Canterbury*, ed. by R. Allers, pp. 172 ff.

[39] In this connection we must consider what Anselm himself says in the *Proslogion* (chap. 4): "A matter is thought one way when the *word* denoting it is thought, and a *different way* when what the *matter* is, is thought. In the former way one can certainly think that God is not, but in the latter way one cannot do so at all." Thus, one can think: a circular

square, yet it still remains questionable whether one is not really thinking only the *words*.

[40] Cf. Gilson, *History*, p. 133.

[41] *Sämtl. Werke*, Vol. 19, p. 168.

[42] C. Nink, *Philosophische Gotteslehre* (München, 1950), p. 137.

[43] A. Stolz, *"Zur Theologie Anselms im Proslogion." Catholica*, 2 Jg. (1933), pp. 1-24.

[44] Ibid., p. 4.

[45] For example, A. Koyré, *L'Idée de Dieu dans la philosophie de St. Anselme* (Paris, 1923), p. 195: The *Proslogion* "is written by a monk for monks, for believers. . . . It does not aim to convert anyone." Similarly, A. Jacquin, *"Les rationes necessariae de St. Anselme." Mélanges Mandonnet* II (1929), pp. 67 ff.

[46] *Fides quaerens intellectum*, p. 199.

[47] *Proslogion*, prooem.

[48] *Proslogion*, cap. 4 (end).

[49] *Fides quaerens intellectum*, p. 199.

[50] *Meditationes de Prima Philosophia*. Appendix to the second replies, paragraph I.—*Principia Philosophiae* I, 14—*Discours de la Méthode*, chap. 4.

[51] *Discours*, chap. 4.

[52] *Quaest. disp. de veritate* 10, 12; *Summa contra Gentes* 1, 10-11; *Summa theologica* I, 2, 1; Commentary on Boethius, *De trinitate* 1, 3.

[53] *Quaest. disp. de veritate* 10, 12.

[54] A. Stolz, loc. cit., p. 4.

[55] *Critique of Pure Reason*, p. 568.

[56] *Quaest. disp. de veritate* 10, 12 ad 2.

[57] Ibid., 10, 12 ad 3 in contr.

[58] Ibid., 10, 12 ad 6.

[59] *Proslogion*, cap. 4.

V

[1] E. Gilson, *Héloïse et Abélard* (Paris, 1948).

[2] Abälard, *Die Leidensgeschichte und der Briefwechsel mit*

Heloise. Ed. by E. Brost. 2 ed. (Heidelberg, 1954), p. 36.

3 Gilson, *Héloïse et Abélard.*

4 Migne, *Patrologia Latina* 178, 113-182.

5 Gilson, *Héloïse et Abélard.*

6 *Leidensgeschichte,* p. 18.

7 Ibid., p. 126.

8 Ibid., p. 95.

9 Gilson has shown that the authenticity of this correspondence cannot really be challenged; the arguments against it are quite inadequate. "The most persuasive and cleverest of all [the hypotheses] remains the assumption that Héloïse was the author of Héloïse's letters and Abélard the author of Abélard's letters." Gilson, *Héloïse et Abélard.*

10 Cf. *Leidensgeschichte,* pp. 143 f.

11 *Leidensgeschichte,* pp. 99, 129, 163, 83.

12 Thus on Anselm of Laon; *Leidensgeschichte,* p. 15.

13 Ibid., p. 64.

14 Ibid., p. 64.

15 Ibid., p. 76.

16 Gilson, *Héloïse et Abélard.*

17 *Leidensgeschichte,* pp. 75 f.

18 In the epistolary tractate sent in 1140 to Pope Innocent II: *Contra quaedam capitula errorum Abaelardi* (Epistola 190). Migne, *Patrologia Latina* 182, 1055.

19 Gilson, *Héloïse et Abélard.*

20 *Leidensgeschichte,* pp. 456 f.

21 Ibid., p. 464.

22 Ibid., pp. 110 f.

23 Migne, *Patrologia Latina* 178, 103.

24 Grabmann, *Scholast. Methode* II, p. 175.

25 *Leidensgeschichte,* p. 8.

26 Überweg-Geyer, p. 216.

27 Cf. Boethius, *Commentaria in Porphyrium a se translatum.* Migne, *Patrologia Latina* 64, 71-158.

28 Überweg-Geyer, p. 216.

29 Cf. I. M. Bochenski, *Formale Logik* (Freiburg-Munich, 1956), pp. 169 f, 219.

[30] *Scito te ipsum,* cap. 14. Migne, *Patrologia Latina* 178, 657.

[31] *Theologia Christiana.* Migne, *Patrologia Latina* 178, 1172.

[32] *Summa theologica* II, II, 2, 7 ad 3. Cf. also *Quaest. disp. de veritate* 14, 11 ad 5.

[33] A. Dempf, *"Die geistige Stellung Bernhards von Clairvaux gegen die cluniazensische Kunst."* In: *Die Chimäre seines Jahrhunderts,* ed. by J. Spörl (Würzburg, 1956), p. 33.

[34] *Theologia Christiana.* Migne, *Patrologia Latina* 178, 1144 ff. Cf. also *In Epist. ad Romanos.* Migne, ibid., 178, 803.

[35] Cf. Grabmann, *Scholast. Methode* II, p. 198.

[36] Ibid., II, 179 f.

[37] *Leidensgeschichte,* pp. 38 f.

[38] Gilson, *Héloïse et Abélard.*

[39] Cf. Arno Borst, *"Abälard und Bernhard."* Historische Zeitschrift, Vol. 186 (1958).

[40] *Divine Comedy;* Paradise, Canto 32.

[41] *Vita* cap. 8, no. 41. Migne, *Patrologia Latina* 185, 251.

[42] *Epistola* 250 (written between 1147 and 1150). Migne, *Patrologia Latina* 182, 451.

[43] *Vereor omnia opera mea et quod operor, non intelligo. Epistola* 306. Migne, *Patrologia Latina* 182, 509.

[44] While Überweg-Geyer (p. 256) says that "no threads lead to Pseudo-Dionysius" from Bernard, Gilson (*History,* p. 164) maintains that Bernard was acquainted both with the works of Dionysius and with the commentaries of Maximus the Confessor, and perhaps even with the writings of John the Scot.

[45] *Serm.* 36. Migne, *Patrologia Latina* 183, 968.

[46] *Sermones.* Migne, *Patrologia Latina* 183, 407.

[47] *Sermo in Nativitate S. Joannis Baptistae,* 3. Migne, *Patrologia* 183, 399. The frequently quoted saying, "Burning is more than knowing," is not authentic.

[48] *Sermones in Canticum* 85 and 86. Migne, *Patrologia Latina* 183, 1187 ff.

[49] Ibid., 85, 14. Migne, *Patrologia Latina* 183, 1194.

[50] De Wulf, *Histoire* (Engl. translation), I, p. 226.

[51] Gilson, *History,* p. 154.

[52] *Metalogicus* 2, 10. Migne, *Patrologia Latina* 199, 869.
[53] *Polycraticus* 7, 2. Migne, *Patrologia Latina* 199, 638 f.
[54] *Metalogicus* 2, 20. Migne, *Patrologia Latina* 199, 881.

VI

[1] *De reductione artium ad theologiam*, cap. 5. *Opera Omnia*, Tom. 5 (Quaracchi, 1891), p. 321.
[2] The reference is to Hugh's pupil and successor, Richard of Saint-Victor.
[3] The word "sacrament" here has the sense of "mystery"; thus we find (Migne, *Patrologia Latina* 176, 803) *sacramentum Trinitatis* and *sacramentum resurrectionis* spoken of.
[4] Cf. André Forest, *De Jean Scot Érigène*, p. 151—Grabmann, *Scholast. Methode* II, 222 ff.
[5] Migne, *Patrologia Latina* 176, 183 f.
[6] O. Zöckler, Art. *"Hugo von St. Victor."* *Realenzyklopädie für prot. Theologie und Kirche* (3rd ed.), Vol. 8, p. 436.
[7] Gilson, *History*, p. 170.
[8] *Didascalia* 2, 1. Migne, *Patrologia Latina* 176, 751.
[9] Ibid., 6, 3; Migne, *Patrologia Latina* 176, 800.
[10] Cf. Grabmann, *Scholast. Methode* II, 229 f.
[11] A. Dempf, *Die Hauptform mittelalterlicher Weltanschauung* (1926), p. 108.
[12] A. Forest, *De Jean Scot Érigène*, p. 150.
[13] A. Dempf has spoken of the "traditionalistic" phase between 600 and 1200, in which what took place was "almost pure reception." *Die Hauptform*, pp. 61 f.
[14] Überweg-Geyer, p. 273.
[15] "Abélard wanted to demonstrate *ad oculos* that not every quotation from the Fathers should be regarded, unexamined and untested, as an unconditionally binding *auctoritas.*" Grabmann, *Scholast. Methode* II, p. 210.
[16] Cf. Josef Pieper, *Hinführung zu Thomas von Aquin*, pp. 77 ff.
[17] Grabmann uses this word "propaganda"; *Scholast. Methode* II, p. 406.

[18] Überweg-Geyer, p. 275.

[19] R. Seeberg, Art. "Lombardus." *Realenzyklopädie für protestantische Theologie und Kirche* (3rd ed.), Vol. 11, p. 641.

[20] R. Wernle, *Einführung in das theologische Studium* (Tübingen, 1908), p. 228.

[21] *Relatorem invenio, non assertorem.* Quoted in A. Forest, *De Jean Scot Érigène*, pp. 158, 160.

[22] A. Dempf, *Die Hauptform*, pp. 108 f.

[23] Cf. Grabmann, *Scholast. Methode* II, 385 f.

[24] *De doctrina Christiana* 1, 2.

[25] Cf. commentary on the Sentences 1 d. 2 divisio textus.

[26] Cf. Grabmann, *Scholast. Methode* II, 364 ff.

[27] Ibid., II, 392.

[28] Ibid., II, 392.

VII

[1] Van Steenberghen, *Le XIIIe siècle*, p. 189.

[2] The "Categories" and "Peri hermeneias."

[3] Cf. Grabmann, *Mittelalterl. Geistesleben* II, p. 66.

[4] The two *"Analytics,"* the *Topics*, the *Sophistic Refutations*.

[5] *Sic et non*, prolog. Migne, *Patrologia Latina* 178, 1349.

[6] Cf. the exact dates in van Steenberghen, *Le XIIIe siècle*, p. 183.

[7] Gilson, *History*, p. 179.

[8] See Chapter V, pp. 91 ff.

[9] See Chapter II, p. 41.

[10] Cf. Böhner, *Christl. Philosophie*, p. 402.

[11] Cf. Gilson, *History*, p. 226. Überweg-Geyer, p. 309.

[12] Böhner, *Christl. Philosophie*, p. 406.

[13] Van Steenberghen, *Le XIIIe siècle*, p. 189.

[14] Ibid.

[15] M. Horten in the *Zeitschrift der deutschen Morgenländischen Gesellschaft*, Vol. 66 (1912), p. 754.

[16] Überweg-Geyer, p. 310.

[17] Nevertheless Roger Bacon, Albertus Magnus, and Thomas

178

Aquinas complained about the inadequacy of the translations (cf. M. Horten, *Zeitschrift der deutschen Morgenländischen Gesellschaft,* Vol. 66 (1912), p. 754. Corrections (for example, by William of Moerbecke) were soon undertaken on the basis of the Greek texts, or in some cases new translations directly from the Greek.

[18] W. von Hertz, *Gesammelte Schriften* (Stuttgart, 1905), p. 161.

[19] Cf. the detailed survey in Steenberghen, *Le XIIIe siècle,* pp. 191-96, 239-42.

[20] *Le XIIIe siècle,* p. 242.

VIII

[1] Grabmann, *Mittelalterl. Geistesleben* II, 70.

[2] "In his Aristotle studies he was, in fact, largely self-taught." Überweg-Geyer, p. 403.

[3] Grabmann, *Mittelalterl. Geistesleben* II, 357.

[4] Commentary on Aristotelian Physics I, 1, 1. *Opera Omnia* (Borgnet) 3, p. 2.

[5] See Chapter II, p. 30.

[6] Commentary on the letters of Dionysius the Areopagite 7, 2. B. *Opera Omnia* (Borgnet) 14, p. 910.

[7] Read, for example, his letters to the Prioress Diana d'Andalò in *To Heaven with Diana!,* Trans. by Gerald Vann, O.P. (Pantheon, New York; Collins, London; 1960.)

[8] B. Geyer, *Albertus Magnus.* In: *Die Grossen Deutschen* (ed. by H. Heimpel, Th. Heuss, B. Reifenberg), Vol. I (Berlin, 1956), p. 201.

[9] The Pope's letter of January 5, 1260, is reprinted in Thomas Ripoll, *Bullarium Ordinis Fratrum Praedicatorum* (Rome, 1729), Vol. I, p. 387. The letter of the general of the order is reproduced in H. Chr. Scheeben, *Albert der Grosse. Zur Chronologie seines Lebens* (Vechta and Leipzig, 1931), pp. 154 ff.

[10] His last will is an indication of this, for he makes disposition not only of his books, but also of gold, silver, and precious

stones. In the will he states expressly: "All know and it can in no wise be doubted that by reason of the exemption from the rule of the order [*ratione exemptionis ab ordine*], granted me by the Pope, I possess temporal goods as my own property and may dispose of them as I think best. . . ." *Testamentum domini Alberti*. Edited by Schmeller in *Gelehrte Anzeigen*, published by members of the Royal Bavarian Academy of Sciences. Vol. 30 (Munich, 1850), Col. 45-47.

[11] B. Geyer, *Albertus Magnus*, p. 210.

[12] Grabmann, *Mittelalterl. Geistesleben* II, 345.

[13] B. Geyer, *Albertus Magnus*, p. 207.

[14] Grabmann, *Mittelalterl. Geistesleben* II, 348.

[15] Überweg-Geyer, p. 410; van Steenberghen, *Le XIIIe siècle*, p. 246.

[16] J. Bernhart, *Albertus Magnus*. In: *Die Grossen Deutschen*, ed. by W. Andreas and W. von Scholz, Vol. I (Berlin, 1935), p. 228.

[17] Ibid., p. 228.

[18] Grabmann, *Mittelalterl. Geistesleben* II, 346.

[19] Böhner, *Christl. Philosophie*, pp. 451 f.

[20] Ibid., p. 470.

[21] *De vegetabilibus*. Ed. C. Jessen, Berlin, 1867.

[22] *De animalibus*. Ed. H. Stadler, two volumes: Münster, 1916, 1920.

[23] In a letter written from Rome to Herder and his wife, Goethe says: "My practice of seeing and reading all things as they are, my fidelity in letting the eye be my guide, my complete abandonment of all pretensions, very quietly keep me happy here." (Nov. 10, 1786.)

[24] *De vegetabilibus* VI, 1; cap. 25; §129, p. 402.

[25] Ibid., IV, 2; cap. 4; §84, pp. 252 f.

[26] *De animalibus* VIII, 4; cap. 1; §134 ff., pp. 628 ff.

[27] *De vegetabilibus* II, 1; cap. 3; §31, pp. 114 f.

[28] *De animalibus* IV, 2; cap. 7; §71, p. 390.

[29] Ibid., VII, 1; cap. 3; §26, p. 506.

[30] For example he contends (Meteor III, 4; cap. 11; *Opera Omnia* [Borgnet] 4, p. 679) that it is not true that the lunar

rainbow appears only twice in fifty years; rather, it is a fact of experience that it has appeared twice in the same year (*veridici experimentatores experti sunt*).

[31] *De vegetabilibus* VI, 1; cap. 1; §1, p. 339.

[32] *De animalibus* XXIII; cap. 24; §110, p. 1493.

[33] *De vegetabilibus* II, 2; cap. 6; §135, p. 157.

[34] H. Stadler in *Verhandlungen deutscher Naturforscher und Ärzte* I (Leipzig, 1909), p. 35.

[35] Albert speaks of the plants with which he intends to deal. "Of those we intend to discuss, some we know from our own experience [*ipsi nos experimento probavimus*]; concerning others we have the accounts of men who, we have learned, say nothing lightly unless it is confirmed by experience [*experimentum*]. For in such matters experience alone affords certainty." *De vegetabilibus* VI, 1; cap. 1; §1, pp. 339 f.

[36] Commentary on Aristotle's *Metaphysics* 1, 1; cap. 2. *Opera Omnia* (Borgnet) 6, 6.

[37] *Ego tales logicas consequentias in scientiis de rebus abhorreo.* Ibid.

[38] W. Heisenberg, *"Das Naturbild der heutigen Physik."* In: *Die Künste im technischen Zeitalter* (Darmstadt, 1956), p. 32.

[39] Thomas Aquinas, *Summa contra Gentes* 2, 4 (1).

[40] B. Geyer, *Albertus Magnus*, p. 212.

[41] Gilson, *History*, p. 289.

[42] Ibid., p. 278.

[43] Van Steenberghen, *Le XIIIe siècle*, p. 239.

IX

[1] Josef Pieper, *Hinführung zu Thomas von Aquin*, p. 183.

[2] Gilson, *History*, p. 325.

[3] Letter of June 1, 1285, to the Bishop of Lincoln. *Registrum epistolarum Johannis Pecham.* Ed. C. T. Martin, three volumes (London, 1882-1885), Vol. III, p. 871.

[4] Cf. van Steenberghen, *Le XIIIe siècle*, p. 300. He also speaks of "Néo-Augustinisme" (p. 296).

[5] Ibid., pp. 218, 229; cf. also Gilson, *History*, pp. 404 f.

[6] *Quaest. disp. de veritate* 14, 9 ad 8.

[7] *Summa contra Gentes* 2, 3.

[8] *Contra impugnantes* 3, 4; no. 400. Cf. also Josef Pieper, *Hinführung zu Thomas von Aquin*, pp. 209, 216.

[9] Cf. also the letters of John Peckham referring to this dispute, published by Fr. Ehrle in *Zeitschrift für Katholische Theologie*, Jg. 13 (1889).

[10] Cf. Josef Pieper, *Thomas-Brevier*, Latin-German (Kösel Verlag, Munich, 1956), pp. 30 ff.

[11] P. Mandonnet makes use of this epithet in the title of his book on Siger of Brabant: *Siger de Brabant et l'averroïsme latin au XIIIe siècle*, 2nd ed., Louvain, 1908-11. Van Steenberghen, who has likewise published extensive studies on Siger of Brabant, comments in this connection: "*L'averroïsme latin du XIIIe siècle est un produit de l'imagination de Renan.*" *Le XIIIe siècle*, p. 280.

[12] Thus van Steenberghen, *Le XIIIe siècle*, pp. 277-83.

[13] Thus Gilson (*History*, p. 408) and Chenu (Introduction, p. 34).

[14] Van Steenberghen says that Siger of Brabant attempted, on the basis of the condemnations, to bring his theses more into harmony with the Credo. Cf. *Le XIIIe siècle*, p. 275.

[15] According to P. Mandonnet (*Siger de Brabant* etc., Vol. I, p. 109, Note 1) this sermon was given in July, 1270. The text may be found in the *Opera Omnia* (ed. Fretté, Paris, 1879), Vol. 32, p. 676.

[16] Van Steenberghen, *Le XIIIe siècle*, p. 276.

[17] Gilson, *History*, pp. 398, 404.

[18] In addition to the above-mentioned book by Pierre Mandonnet I should also mention Fernand van Steenberghen, *Siger de Brabant d'après ses oeuvres inédites*. Two volumes, Louvain, 1931, 1942.

[19] Chenu, Introduction, pp. 29, 30.

[20] Van Steenberghen, *Le XIIIe siècle*, pp. 271, 272, 280.

[21] Ibid., pp. 268-70.

[22] *"Ce solitaire n'a pas écrit pour son siècle."* Gilson, *La Philosophie au moyen âge*, 2nd ed., Paris, 1944, p. 590.
[23] Gilson, *History*, p. 409. Cf. also Steenberghen, *Le XIIIe siècle*, p. 296.
[24] *On the Singularity of the Intellect; On the Eternity of the World.*
[25] Cf. van Steenberghen, *Le XIIIe siècle*, p. 276.
[26] Ibid., p. 272.
[27] Ibid.
[28] Commentary on Aristotle, *De caelo* I, 22.

X

[1] Überweg-Geyer, pp. 493, 495.
[2] Chapter V: *"Autour de la condamnation de 1277."* *Le XIIIe siècle*, pp. 289-322.
[3] Ibid., p. 302.
[4] Ibid., p. 287.
[5] Gilson, *History*, pp. 385, 408, 465.
[6] Van Steenberghen, *Le XIIIe siècle*, p. 268.
[7] Ibid., p. 302.
[8] Gilson, *History*, p. 728.
[9] Van Steenberghen, *Le XIIIe siècle*, p. 302.
[10] *"Dicunt enim ea esse vera secundum philosophiam, sed non secundum fidem catholicam, quasi sint duae contrariae veritates."* P. Mandonnet, *Siger de Brabant* II, p. 175.
[11] Van Steenberghen, *Le XIIIe siècle*, p. 305.
[12] The letter has been edited by Fr. Ehrle (*Archiv für Literatur und Kirchengeschichte des Mittelalters*, Vol. 5, pp. 614 ff.) and A. Birkenmajer (*Beiträge zur Geschichte der Philosophie des Mittelalters*, Vol. 20, 5).
[13] P. Glorieux, Article "Tempier" in *Dictionnaire de Théologie Catholique*, Vol. XV, 1, col. 102.
[14] *Les Oeuvres et la doctrine de Siger de Brabant* (Brussels, 1938), p. 183.
[15] I. M. Bochenski, *Der sowjetrussische dialektische Materialismus* (Berne, 1950), p. 73.

[16] *Le XIIIe siècle*, p. 304.

[17] Ibid., p. 305.

[18] Gilson, *History*, p. 385.

[19] *Briefwechsel zwischen Wilhelm Dilthey und dem Grafen Paul Yorck von Wartenburg, 1877-1897* (Halle, 1923), p. 126.

[20] Gilson, *History*, pp. 408, 465.

XI

[1] See Chapter IV, p. 60.

[2] *"Necesse est ergo eos de humana, quoniam non est alia de qua possint, natura restaurari." Cur Deus homo* 1, 16.

[3] Ibid.

[4] Ibid.

[5] The figures in parentheses refer to the order of the sentences as given by Mandonnet (*Siger de Brabant* II, pp. 175 ff.).

[6] Gilson, *History*, p. 409.

[7] Ibid., p. 497.

[8] Copleston, p. 477.

[9] Ibid., p. 481.

[10] *"In hoc errabant Philosophi, ponentes omnia quae sunt a Deo immediate, esse ab eo necessario."* Oxon. Prolog. 1; no. 8; *Opera Omnia* (Paris, 1891-95), Vol. 8, p. 15.

[11] Gilson, *History*, p. 452.

[12] *"Nihil aliud a voluntate est causa totalis volitionis in voluntate."* Oxon. 2, 24; no. 22. *Opera*, Vol. 13, p. 221.

[13] ". . . *[voluntas] quae est libera per essentiam."* Oxon. 1, 17, 3; no. 5. *Opera*, Vol. 10, p. 56. *"In voluntate possumus duo considerare, vel inquantum est appetitus, vel inquantum est libera. . . . Ratio . . . formalior voluntatis est magis 'libera' quam ratio 'appetitus.'"* Oxon. 2, 25; no. 16. *Opera*, Vol. 13, p. 210. Cf. Copleston, p. 539.

[14] Thomas Aquinas, *Commentary on the Sentences* 3 d. 1, 1, 3; obj. 1.

[15] Ibid., 3 d. 1, 1, 3; obj. 5.

[16] Ibid., 3 d. 1, 1, 3; obj. 4.

[17] Ibid., 3 d. 1, 1, 3; 3 d. 1, 1, 2.

[18] Böhner, *Christl. Philosophie,* pp. 559, 564.

[19] Gilson, *History,* p. 465.

[20] Ibid., p. 409.

[21] *"Au lendemain des évènements de 1277, l'école franciscaine prend la tête du mouvement doctrinal."* Van Steenberghen, *Le XIIIe siècle,* p. 306.

[22] Thomas Aquinas, *Commentary on the Sentences* 3 d. 1, 1, 2.

[23] *". . . simpliciter destruere vel annihilare."* Reportata Parisiensia 4 d. 43, 2 ad 7. *Opera,* Vol. 24, p. 497.

[24] J. Hirschberger, *Geschichte der Philosophie* (Freiburg, 1949), Vol. I, p. 458.

[25] E. Hochstetter, "Nominalismus?" *Franciscan Studies,* Vol. 9 (1949), p. 396.

[26] Gilson, *History,* p. 501.

[27] *Commentary on the Sentences* 4 qu. 9 E.

[28] *Centilogium theologicum,* concl. 6.

[29] *Quaest. disp. de Potentia Dei* 5, 4 ad 10.

[30] Ibid., 5, 4.

[31] *Quaest. quodlibetales* 4, 4.

[32] Gilson, *History,* p. 470.

XII

[1] *Enneads,* I, 6, 8.

[2] *Farbenlehre, Didaktischer Teil,* Einleitung. Ed. by G. Ipsen. (Insel-Verlag, Leipzig), p. 36.

[3] It is nevertheless interesting that of all people the "modern," the "Averroistic" Aristotelians are the ones who defend the master's doctrines against the new physics "with far more tenacity than the orthodox theologians themselves"; "philosophically speaking, it is Averroism, and not scholasticism in general, that deserves to be called a repetitious and obdurate Aristotelianism." Gilson, *History,* p. 522.

[4] The series "Great Books of the Western World," edited by R. M. Hutchins and issued by the publishers of the *Encyclopaedia Britannica* (54 volumes in all), is provided with a key

that is thoroughly "scholastic" and, so it seems to me, peda-. gogically excellent, entitled *The Great Ideas. A Syntopicon of Great Books of the Western World*. Ed. by M. J. Adler and W. Gorman (Chicago, London, Toronto, 1952).

[5] T. S. Eliot, "Modern Education and the Classics." *Selected Essays* (London, 1951), pp. 515 f.

[6] The same complex organization may be discerned in the work of Plato, whose philosophy likewise rested upon the marriage of mythical tradition and rational understanding. Wherever Plato speaks of life after death, for example in the dialogues *Gorgias* and *Phaedo*, he treats the subject in a three-fold way, and each approach is quite distinct: simple relating of the mythical tale (of the judgment of the dead); the "theological" interpretation of this story (*Gorgias* 524 b 1); and then the harmonizing of that theological interpretation with the empirical knowledge of the earth and the cosmos accepted by his time (*Phaedo* 108 c ff.). It is clear that setting up a simple opposition between the non-Christian and the "Middle Ages" is insufficient; we must go much further in establishing our contrasts.

[7] Thomas Aquinas, *Summa theologica,* prologus.

[8] Chenu, Introduction, p. 291.

[9] *"Quia . . . Mahumetistae et pagani non conveniunt nobiscum in auctoritate alicujus Scripturae, per quam possint convinci . . . necesse est ad naturalem rationem recurrere, cui omnes assentire coguntur."* Summa contra Gentes 1, 2.

[10] Cf. Josef Pieper, *Hinführung zu Thomas von Aquin,* pp. 209, 216.

[11] Pierre Teilhard de Chardin, *Lettres de voyage 1923-1939* (Paris, 1956).

[12] Ibid.

[13] Cf. Josef Pieper, *Gibt es eine nicht-christliche Philosophie? Weistum, Dichtung, Sakrament* (Kösel Verlag, Munich, 1954), pp. 51 ff.

*Only matters mentioned in the text
are included*

430 Augustine dies in his episcopal seat of Hippo Regius while the city is being besieged by the Vandals.

431 Council of Ephesus. Condemnation of the Christological doctrine of Nestorius. Emigration of the Aristotelians.

480 Boethius born in Rome.

493 Founding of the Ostrogothic Kingdom in Italy.

before 500 Presumable date of the writings of Dionysius the Areopagite.

525 Execution of Boethius.

529 Closing of the Platonic Academy in Athens. Founding of Monte Cassino by Benedict of Nursia.

540 Cassiodorus resigns his political office and withdraws to the monastery of Vivarium.

553 End of the Ostrogothic Kingdom in Italy.

568 Founding of the Lombard Kingdom in Italy.

571 Mohammed born in Mecca.

635 Beginning of the Arab conquests (Persia, Egypt).

668 Theodore, born in Tarsus, becomes Archbishop of Canterbury and establishes classical studies in the British Isles.

711 Beginning of the Mohammedan conquest of Spain.

732 In the Battle of Poitiers Charles Martel throws the Arabs into retreat.

circa 810 John the Scot born in Ireland.

circa	830	Hilduin, Abbot of Saint-Denis, writes the *Vita S. Dionysii*.
	980	Avicenna born in the Persian province of Bokhara.
circa	1010	Lanfranc born in Pavia.
	1033	Anselm of Canterbury born in Aosta.
	1037	Death of Avicenna in Hamadan.
	1066	Battle of Hastings. Norman Conquest of England.
	1079	Abélard born near Nantes.
	1085	Liberation of Toledo from Moorish dominion.
	1091	Bernard of Clairvaux born near Dijon.
	1096	Hugh of Saint-Victor born at Hartingam in the Harz Mountains.
before	1100	Arnold of Brescia born.
after	1100	Peter Lombard born in Novara.
	1101	Héloïse born in Paris.
	1109	Death of Anselm of Canterbury.
circa	1115	John of Salisbury born.
	1126	Averroës born at Córdoba.
	1126	Raymond of Sauvetât becomes Archbishop of Toledo, founds the school of translators at Toledo.
	1135	Moses Maimonides born at Córdoba.
	1141	Death of Hugh of Saint-Victor in Paris.
	1142	Death of Abélard at Cluny.
	1153	Death of Bernard of Clairvaux.
	1160	Death of Peter Lombard in Paris.
circa	1170	Dominic born in Calaroga (Castile).
	1180	Death of John of Salisbury in Chartres.
	1182	Francis of Assisi born in Assisi.
circa	1197	Albertus Magnus born in Lauingen (Swabia).
	1198	Death of Averroës.
before	1200	Jordan of Saxony born in Borgberge near Dassel.
	1204	Death of Moses Maimonides.

1210	First ecclesiastical ban on Aristotle pronounced at Paris.
1221	Death of Dominic in Bologna.
1221	Bonaventura born at Viterbo.
circa 1225	Thomas Aquinas born in Roccasecca.
1226	Death of Francis of Assisi in Assisi.
1237	Death of Jordan of Saxony near Acre.
circa 1240	Siger of Brabant born in the diocese of Liége.
circa 1240	John Peckham born.
1266	Duns Scotus born in Scotland.
1274	Death of Thomas Aquinas in Fossanuova.
1274	Death of Bonaventura at Lyons during the council.
1277	Condemnation of extreme Aristotelianism at Paris and Oxford.
1280	Death of Albertus Magnus in Cologne.
circa 1280	Marsilius of Padua born in Padua.
1282	Death of Siger of Brabant in Orvieto.
1292	Death of John Peckham in Canterbury.
before 1300	William of Ockham born near London.
1308	Death of Duns Scotus in Cologne.
1343	Death of Marsilius of Padua in Munich.
1349	Death of William of Ockham in Munich.

INDEX

Abélard, 30, 77f, 79ff, 88, 96f,
101, 136, 174f, 177
Agapetus, Pope, 41
Alaric, 19
Albertus Magnus, 24, 48, 76,
109ff, 124, 134, 178
Alcuin, 20, 44, 48, 50
Alexander IV, Pope, 111
Alexander of Hales, 76
Alexandria, 41, 44
Allers, R., 173
America, 153f
Anselm of Canterbury, 46, 55ff,
78, 85, 90, 94, 136, 172, 173f
Arabs, 101f, 112
Archimedes, 103
Aristotle, 24, 28, 30, 44, 76, 100ff,
104, 123
Arnold of Brescia, 82
Augustine, 19, 20, 21, 24, 48, 52,
60, 61, 98, 102, 112f, 123
Averroës, 104f
Avicenna, 104, 106, 112

Baeumker, Cl., 167
Baghdad, 104
Barth, K., 67, 71
Benedict of Nursia, 17, 26
Bernard of Clairvaux, 77, 82f,
87ff, 94, 176
Bernhart, J., 113
Bochenski, J. M., 175
Böhner, Ph., 165
Boethius, 20, 21, 26ff, 44, 53, 60,
72, 78, 85, 100, 109, 118, 123,
136
Bonaventura, 11, 38ff, 71, 76, 78,
94, 112, 120
"Books of sentences," 95
Borst, A., 176

Canterbury, 58
Cassiodorus, 40ff, 103, 155
Chebu, M.-D., 167
Christian philosophy, 17, 156ff,
162
Cîteaux, 87
Clement of Alexandria, 19, 86
Cluny, 57, 83, 87
Copleston, Fr., 165
Córdoba, 104
Creation, 116

Dante, 32
Dempf, A., 176, 177
Descartes, 15, 65, 67, 71f, 75, 76
Dilthey, W., 135
Dionysius Areopagita, 46ff, 55,
89, 94, 101f, 112, 139, 172, 176
Dominicus Gondisalvi, 106
"Double truth," 122f, 129, 146
Duns Scotus, 76, 78f, 99, 136,
139ff, 148

Eadmer, 56f, 59, 65
Edessa, 103
Eliot, T. S., 156
Emigration, 103
Ephesus, Council of (431), 103
Epicurus, 19
Eternity, 31
Euclid, 103
Experience, 91, 93, 114, 115f,
149, 181

Fideism, 73
Fides implicita, 86
Forest, A., 166
Francis de Sales, St., 49
"Free area," 40, 155f, 169
Freedom, 35, 139ff, 146, 148